Sheriff's Son

Lessons Learned

by

Wayne Skarka

with

Sheriff Donald "Butch" Campsey, Ret.

Black Rose Writing

www.blackrosewriting.com

The final approval for this literary material is granted by the author.

First printing

All work cited and documented based on factual accounts.

ISBN: 978-1-935605-32-4

PUBLISHED BY BLACK ROSE WRITING

www.blackrosewriting.com

Printed in the United States of America

The Sheriff's Son is printed in 12-point Times New Roman

A TRUE STORY

TABLE OF CONTENTS

About the Author

Wayne Skarka began his career as a police investigator when he entered the U.S. Army in 1972. He was assigned as a military police specialist, stationed at Fort Hood, Texas, where he completed two years of active military service. Later, he served in the National Guard. In 1974, Wayne worked briefly for the Killeen, Texas Police Department. He graduated from Central Texas College in 1976.

After graduation, Wayne worked as a police officer in the small central Texas community of Rockdale. In 1978, Wayne joined the Lake Jackson, Texas Police Department and a few months later transferred to the Brazoria County, Texas Sheriff's Department. After one year, he was promoted to sergeant in the Criminal Investigations Unit. While assigned as an investigator, he began his thirty-year pursuit of working for justice for families all across Texas grieving the murders of young girls.

In 1980, Wayne returned to his family roots in northern California, where he was hired by the San Mateo Police Department in the Patrol Division. He later worked in the Vice Narcotics and Detective units.

Wayne was active in the Police Association, serving three terms as the president of the San Mateo Police Officers Association. Wayne was also elected to the California Organization of Police and Sheriff's, a statewide association representing thousands of California police officers.

In 1989, Wayne retired from active law enforcement after a service-related injury to his back. Since then, he has operated a large statewide private investigation company. Wayne's company, Warrant Investigations, Inc., specializes in the investigation of fraud related to workers' compensation injuries.

Wayne is divorced and lives in the Sacramento area. He has two grown children, Kimberly, age twenty-four, and Michael, age twenty.

FORWARD
Sheriff Donald "Butch" Campsey, Ret.

I was born and raised in Medina County, Texas. My father migrated here after the Great Depression and married my mother. They raised twelve children in the small community of Devine. We were a close family. In February 1961, I had no idea that the disappearance and murder of fourteen-year-old Claudette "Carolyn" Covey would play such an important part in my adult life. I still remember the day in 1961 when a sheriff's deputy came to our house. I was thirteen. The deputy asked to borrow a set of two-way radios we had received as Christmas presents. The walkie-talkies were to be used to assist volunteers searching for Carolyn. I also remember the day when Carolyn's body was found.

I grew up listening to stories and rumors of what may have happened to Carolyn. The most often repeated theory was that County Sheriff Charlie Hitzfelder Sr., or members of his family, may have been involved in her death. The talk around town was that the sheriff's son was dating Carolyn, and that his father objected strongly.

I attended college and studied criminal justice. After graduation, I went to work for the Texas Department of Public Safety. I completed the Police Academy training and found myself stationed in Medina County. For the next three years, I honed my skills as a state trooper, while Charlie Hitzfelder was our county sheriff.

Growing up, I often heard rumors that Sheriff Hitzfelder was corrupt. When I began working as a state trooper in Medina County, I saw firsthand the corruption surrounding him. The sheriff was a politically powerful man and many citizens feared him.

In 1975, friends convinced me to run for county sheriff. While campaigning, I met Barbara Covey, Carolyn Covey's sister. I asked her to vote for me. Barbara told me that her family believed that Sheriff Hitzfelder or his son was involved in the death of Carolyn. She told me that I would get her vote if I promised to reopen the investigation into her sister's death. I made that promise to Barbara, and a few months later, I was elected sheriff.

One of the first things I did after taking office was to locate the case file of Carolyn Covey's disappearance and murder. I found a cardboard box in a storage room at the Sheriff's Department. The box was labeled with the name Covey. Carolyn's skull and several of her bones were inside. I was stunned. It was sixteen years since her death. Right then and there, I decided to do my best to solve her murder so she could finally be laid to rest. The Covey family needed closure. I took the box with me everywhere I went for the next seven years. I felt that I needed to protect Carolyn.

For the next seven years, my life was consumed with Carolyn's death. I spent many sleepless nights thinking of ways to end the suffering of Carolyn's family. I wanted to bring justice to Carolyn and her family.

I soon learned that I would have to fight the old guard in the county to solve Carolyn's murder. The county commissioners, who controlled the Sheriff's Department budget, refused to supply funds to investigate Carolyn's murder. These weren't the only roadblocks along the way. Many people who knew the Hitzfelders were afraid to talk to me. I did all I could, contacting living witnesses. Some cooperated; some did not. I made progress over the years and formed an opinion as to what happened the night Carolyn went missing.

I served two terms as county sheriff and two terms as county judge. For sixteen years, I tried to solve Carolyn's murder. In the 1990s, both Sheriff Hitzfelder and his son passed away. It was now thirty years since Carolyn's death. Time has a way of dissolving people's memories. Interest in Carolyn's death faded. To this day, many older residents of Medina County have their own theories of what happened to Carolyn.

Thirty-eight years later, Carolyn's death remains the most notorious unsolved murder in our county's history. This book connects the dots and presents the facts surrounding Carolyn's murder in 1961. It also connects the sheriff's son to many similar murders over thirty years throughout Texas.

Claudette Carolyn Covey was finally buried in Devine, Texas on September 23, 1983.

PROLOGUE

Crime Scene Investigation or "CSI", or "The First 48" are some of the popular television programs where viewers witness the aftermath of a murder. After one hour, viewers see the suspect arrested and charged with murder. It is true that current crime forensics offer police the ability to build a criminal case against a murder suspect in short order. Laser technology, computers, DNA, and state-of-the-art crime labs are becoming routine and can actually lead to solving murders in an hour. This was not always the case. Prior to the 1980s, the tools used by law enforcement were archaic by comparison.

In the early 1960s, most murders were solved by eyewitness testimony, confessions or fingerprints. This made it easy for some street-wise criminals to get away with murder. A serial killer, familiar with the ways of law enforcement, could kill again and again.

If the 1960s criminal forensics were familiar to a killer, he would have an advantage over most police agencies in America. In 1961, a serial killer from Medina County, Texas came of age. The first murder may have occurred when fourteen-year-old Claudette Carolyn Covey disappeared on Valentine's night. Claudette's body, ironically, was found nine months later on Halloween evening. The sheriff's son was suspected, but never charged. Claudette's murderer remained a mystery. A new sheriff, Butch Campsey, was elected in 1977 and spent sixteen years trying to solve Claudette's murder. For eight years he served as sheriff, followed by eight years as the Medina County judge. Sheriff Campsey no longer works in law enforcement. He is a special education teacher, working with troubled pre-teen boys.

Judge Campsey decided to leave politics to pursue a new career to better support his large family. In 1992, he began a business dealing with the incarceration of youthful offenders. After a few years, he decided to pursue his real passion of helping troubled kids.

The Sheriff's Son will explore the life of Charlie James Hitzfelder Jr., the son of Sheriff Charles Hitzfelder Sr. "Junior," as some called him, died of cancer in 1998 and may have gotten away with the murder of several young women due to the protection of his powerful father.

In Texas, immense political power is wielded by county sheriffs. These men are forces to be reckoned with. Political parties elect county sheriffs, and once elected, they insure their re-elections by maintaining their political machines.

In the 1950s, a few Texas county sheriffs were so politically powerful they had the ability, if they chose to do so, to engage in corrupt practices with impunity. By no means were all sheriffs corrupt. Only a small percentage of these men took this course. Such was the case of Medina County Sheriff Charles J. Hitzfelder Sr. Medina County has a population of less than 45,000 and is located in Texas' southwestern hill country about thirty miles west of San Antonio. The county seat, Hondo, was the base of operations for Sheriff Charlie's twenty-four-year reign of terror.

In early 1960, Charlie's eighteen-year-old son, Charlie Jr., was dating two very young girls, Mary Ruth Cadenhead, fourteen, from nearby Devine, Texas, and Claudette Carolyn Covey, thirteen. Carolyn was from Hondo. Charlie objected to Junior dating girls that were below his own standards. A girl like Carolyn, from a poor family was definitely out of the question.

Charlie Sr. demanded over and over again that Charlie Jr. straighten up his life after several brushes with law enforcement. In October 1961, one of Charlie's deputies caught Junior drinking beer. This deputy was said to be having an affair with Junior's mother, Iona. Rumors of the affair had spread around town. The sheriff, who must have known about her infidelity, never confronted Iona about her unfaithfulness. The sheriff's deputy telephoned Iona to tell her of Junior's latest brush with the law.

Iona, like her husband, was fed up with Junior's misdeeds. She knew that her husband's reputation was everything to him. It was important that the Hitzfelder family be seen as a respectable family. Junior's frequent run-ins with the law had to come to an end. Something had to be done with Junior.

Before Sheriff Charlie and Iona could act, they got the news that Junior's girlfriend, Mary Ruth Cadenhead, was pregnant. The Hitzfelders were furious, while Mary Ruth's parents were devastated. They could not stand Junior. Mary Ruth's father demanded that Junior be arrested for having sex with his minor daughter. The sheriff and Iona did not want Junior to be burdened with a wife and child, but realized they had to act on Mary Ruth's pregnancy. The sheriff decided that Mary Ruth and Junior should get married. The idea of an abortion was out of the question for Mary Ruth. Faced with no other recourse, she agreed to the marriage. Junior was told he had to wed Mary Ruth and then join the Navy. Junior was terribly afraid of his father, knowing what he was capable of doing. Junior agreed to immediately enlist in the Navy and then marry his pregnant girlfriend. Junior left Hondo and went through basic training in San Diego, California. Both families agreed that Mary Ruth would stay with her parents in Devine. Things remained pretty much normal in Hondo until early February 1961.

On Valentine's Day 1961, Claudette Carolyn Covey disappeared from Hondo. Nine months later on Halloween Day, her remains were found. Carolyn's body had been dumped in a field about eight miles from Hondo, near the small community of Yancey. Carolyn had died from two shots to the head. Even before her body was discovered, rumors had begun to circulate that Carolyn and Junior were involved in a relationship. Some believed Carolyn was pregnant when she disappeared. There was talk in town that Junior was in Hondo—home on leave or AWOL—the day Carolyn went missing. Townspeople had their suspicions, but were powerless to do anything about them because of the sheriff's power. Townsfolk remain suspicious of Carolyn's death to this day. At the time of her murder, some thought the sheriff had Carolyn killed. Almost fifty years later, Carolyn Covey's death remains the most notorious unsolved murder in Medina County history.

This novel chronicles the life of Charlie Hitzfelder Jr. from 1960 to his death by cancer in 1998. In 1963, he was arrested for the rape of a twelve-year-old California girl. In 1976, he was arrested for the forcible rape of his eleven-year-old stepdaughter. In both cases, Charlie Jr. walked away unpunished, largely due to the connections of his powerful father. During his lifetime, Chuck, as he was known later in life, would marry eight times and had one common-law wife.

Charlie's wives never reported any sort of abuse during his lifetime, because of their fears of retribution by Charlie or his father. After Charlie's death many of his wives reported horrific mental and sexual abuse at the hands of their husband. Charlie did not confine his sexual and physical abuse to his wives. Like their mothers, Charlie's stepdaughters feared him and his father. Those fears prevented them from coming forward to report their abuse to their mothers or the police. Charlie Jr. would threaten the lives of the girls' mothers and the lives of those the girls loved. Only after his death would these girls come forward and report the terrible sexual and physical abuse. Charlie was never arrested for domestic violence, which began in 1963. Over the next twenty-five years, Charlie's abuse of his wives and their children continued to escalate. Even after divorce, they remained terrorized by and frightened of Junior.

From 1971 to the early 1990s, Charlie Jr. was a suspect in the murders of many young girls in the Houston/Galveston area of Texas. These unsolved murders are often referred to as the Killing Field Murders or the I-45 Mystery Murders. The modus operandi or method of operation of many of the murders bears a striking similarity to the death of Carolyn Covey. Many of the victims were abducted and taken to rural areas. After being raped, they were shot twice in the head with a small caliber weapon. Their bodies were dumped in fields just off the roadway. It is very likely that Junior. was responsible for many of the murders.

While the one responsible for these murders remains in doubt, the political power of Charlie's father does not. Charlie saved his son from the grasp of the law, over and over again. The protection of his father allowed junior to walk away from justice his entire life.

ONE

This is God's Country
Please Don't Drive Through it Like Hell

The local Lions Club posted a welcoming message in 1930 on a sign along Highway 90 in Hondo, Medina County, Texas. The sign stated, "This is God's country, please don't drive through it like hell". "God's Country" is how the residents of Medina County feel about their home. Hondo is located at the intersection of US 90 and FM 463. Hondo was established in the 1880s along the Southern Pacific Railroad tracks. It is west of Bexar County and forty miles west of San Antonio. Medina County is known for its numerous hunting ranches. Deer and upland game birds are abundant during hunting season. In 1942, the U.S. Army Air Corps constructed the Hondo Army Airfield, which closed down after World War II. For a time, two radar sites remained in operation. Agriculture is the major industry of the county. Forty-five percent of the county is considered prime farmland. Indian corn, sorghum, oats, pecans, and honey are principle crops.

The county's population in the 1950s was under 30,000. Today, Medina County remains small with just over 40,000 residents, 18,000 of which are Hispanic. While modest by population, Medina County is vast in landmass, consisting of 1,300 square miles. Medina Lake Reservoir lies north of Hondo. In 1913, the dam that created the reservoir was the fourth largest in the United States. Eventually, the dam held back enough water to irrigate 60,000 acres. The lake is home to various species of bass, including black and white.

Today, there are only six small communities in Medina

County, including Castroville, Devine, Natalia, D'Hanis, Yancey and Hondo, which has less than 8,000 people. Hondo remains much the same as in the 1950s, a typical small Texas town. In Hondo everyone in town recognizes most residents on sight. Strangers and tourists sometime arouse suspicion. Like most Texas towns in the 1950's, neighborhoods broke down along economic and ethnic lines. This was, and remains the case in Hondo. The neighborhood for poor whites and Hispanics is referred to as "the wrong side of the tracks." Since the early 1960s, the area has improved, but lower-income homes remain. Hondo has about 200 small businesses, including the Raye Theater, which was established decades ago. Today, the Raye Theater looks much the same as it did in the 1960s, showing movies daily. Most of the downtown businesses were constructed of D'Hanis brick. There are twenty-six cemeteries in the county. The newspapers of record are the Medina County News (formally the Quill) established in 1879, and the *Hondo Anvil Herald.*

The Lord High Sheriff
The Devil is in Power in Politics

In the 1950s and through the 1980s, some of the most politically powerful people in Texas were county sheriffs. In Texas, sheriffs are elected by party affiliation. Prior to 1984, politicians were mostly Democrats and most ran formidable political machines, as did some county sheriffs. Sheriff Charlie Hitzfelder Sr. was elected sheriff of Medina County in 1952. He took office in January of 1953. Over the next 24 years, he became infamous. He wielded tremendous political power and was feared not only by criminals, but also by the residents of Medina County. Like most politicians of the time, Hitzfelder knew how to manipulate townsfolk through political favors, keeping them in his debt. Sheriff Charlie knew it was pretty much a sure thing he would be reelected sheriff for life, largely due to his powerful Democrat machine.

Certain county sheriffs stood out as men to be reckoned with. Sheriff Charlie Hitzfelder was such a man. Charlie knew it did not matter how big your county was. Even in a small county, political connections could make you very powerful. Sheriff Charlie enjoyed a special privilege, rarely paying for anything in town, while receiving free food, groceries, gasoline, clothing, and just about any other commodity he desired. No one dared to ask for payment. Throughout Texas, Charlie was known as one of the lord high sheriffs. Not all Texas sheriffs were corrupt by any means, but some thought they were above the law. Prior to his election, Charlie was a thirty-nine-year-old deputy sheriff, working for the Medina County sheriff. Charlie was a stereotypical version of a sheriff, similar to those portrayed in dime novels and Hollywood movies. At six feet tall, Charlie was a slender man with dark brown hair always cut short. He was clean-shaven and only wore his glasses when reading. Charlie had a demanding demeanor, made more prominent by his ever-present Stetson hat. As sheriff, he was a no-nonsense kind of man. Prior to joining the sheriff's department, Charlie had developed a countywide reputation as a coward-a reputation dating back to the late 1940s.

Prior to becoming a deputy sheriff, Charlie owed a local man, Arthur Campsey, money for work done on his farm. One day, Arthur Campsey chased Charlie out the back door of a small beer joint, trying to collect his money. Every time Charlie saw Campsey, he tried to avoid him. One Friday night, Arthur spotted Charlie's car parked in front of the local watering hole and stormed inside to find Charlie sitting at a table with Iona Langford, his future wife. Campsey yelled to Charlie that they were going to settle up right now. Charlie jumped up from his table and ran like hell out the back door. This single act of cowardice cemented Charlie's reputation throughout the county. Years later, after Charlie became sheriff, his reputation as a coward waned. Now people feared Charlie, and he liked that. Charlie's position as a deputy sheriff, his gun, and his ability to lock people up evoked fear. Most townsfolk didn't respect Charlie, but they feared him. In his twenty-four years as sheriff, Charlie was never able to gain the respect of many Medina County citizens.

In 1953, when Charlie took office, there were three deputy sheriffs, including Charlie, working in Medina County. There was not much crime in small Texas counties like Medina, and not much need for many deputies. In Medina County everyone knows one another. Getting away with crime would be quite an accomplishment. Only crimes committed by outsiders went unsolved.

As Charlie grew into the job, he learned his politics well. He soon became a political kingpin in southwestern Texas. Charlie knew almost everyone's little secrets and how to use those secrets to his own advantage. Once Charlie had his political hooks into you, you were in his debt for life. He gained power by either doing you a favor or by finding out about your weaknesses. Either way, Charlie had you for life.

Charlie decided to run for county sheriff early in 1952. Sheriff Jack Fusselman decided not to run for reelection and gave Charlie his blessing. Along with Fusselman's support, Charlie was backed by the county's Democratic political machine. Charlie did not earn political support through his qualifications as a law enforcement officer, but because he knew the secrets of the people who could help him politically. Charlie knew where their skeletons were buried. The primary election in June was a farce. Charlie's handpicked opponent for the Democratic primary agreed to not even try to win. When Charlie took office in January 1953, he called his election a landslide. In reality, there was no real opponent in the general election in November 1952.

Thus began Charlie's twenty-four-year run of corruption, misdeeds, greed, and political influence. From the start of his term, Charlie knew how to ensure an outcome, shaping political and personal outcomes to his liking. If someone strayed from Charlie's plan, the person responsible would live to regret Charlie's unhappiness.

Charles Hitzfelder was born in La Coste, Texas on August 14, 1914. He was an average student and notably unremarkable. In 1950, Charlie took a job as a deputy sheriff with the Medina County Sheriff's Department. Charlie had been on the job for only two years when Sheriff Fusselman decided to retire. The opportunity to run for sheriff became a defining moment in Charlie's life. In his short tenure as a deputy, Charlie had learned well the good old boy system.

Charlie knew that in order to be elected, he would have to make deals with the devil, as well as the town's leading citizens. Charlie was prepared; he had learned his lessons well. For the next twenty-four years, Charlie would remain county sheriff. As elections came and went, Charlie's competition faded away. The lack of challengers was not due to his exemplary police work, but the inherent corruption in the sheriff's office. Charlie became powerful.

In the late 1960s, Charlie arranged to attend the prestigious FBI Academy by pulling some strings in Austin. He took advantage of this opportunity to finally learn police techniques and the law enforcement forensics of the time. Prior to attending the FBI Academy, Charlie had not attended a recognized police academy, as was common for most police officers. Charlie's law enforcement experiences were primarily gained from his day-to-day work as a deputy sheriff. Before the FBI training, Charlie attended a weeklong sheriff's seminar, presented by the Sheriff's Association for newly elected sheriffs. The seminar dealt mostly with the political dos and don'ts for new sheriffs.

Back in 1952, like today, the sheriff runs the county jail. The jail's population was never much more than three or four prisoners. It was common for the sheriff to live at the county jail in special quarters. Charlie and Iona initially lived in the courthouse basement. The sheriff's wife cooked for the prisoners and often babysat the drunks locked up for the night. In 1952 a sheriff's pay was very low. In order to get by, some corrupt sheriffs found illegal ways to make money, like looking the other way when criminal acts were committed. Rarely did anyone in the community have the courage to report suspected misconduct. Shaking down local business owners provided Charlie with a source of income in addition to offering protection for prostitution, illegal gambling, cockfighting, and drug running. It was even rumored throughout the county, that some of the deputies, and perhaps even the sheriff, operated a gun theft ring. These officers were said to confiscate guns from criminals and the public, taking the guns to San Antonio, where they were sold to pawn shops.

Hondo lies about one hundred miles north of the Mexican border along Highway 90 on a direct route to San Antonio. Drug couriers and human smugglers often passed through town, operating with impunity due to deals they made with Sheriff Hitzfelder. Sheriffs like Charlie entered office as poor men, but left with more money than a sheriff's pay would allow. Honest businessmen were afraid to complain about payoffs, and criminals knew that speaking up could bring jail time, or worse. The cycle of corruption continued year after year.

The Sheriff's Family

Charlie's home life, as far as the public knew, was typical of the time. He married Iona Langford in 1941. She was born in 1922 in Devine, Texas. Throughout her life, Iona was a demanding, if attractive, woman of medium height and shapely figure. She always wore glasses. After Charlie was elected sheriff, Iona finally got what she wanted: to be in charge. Being the sheriff's wife was a perfect fit for Iona. Charlie's personality was very similar to Iona's, with one big difference; Charlie would often defer to Iona's judgments and wishes. As sheriff, he would never accommodate anyone. During his twenty-four years as sheriff, Iona was the only person to whom Charlie would sometimes yield.

Iona and Charlie had three children. Charlie Jr., the oldest, was born in August of 1942. Jeanette was born in November 1945. Barbara Ann, the youngest child, was born in November 1948.

In 1961, Charlie Jr. was eighteen years old. He stood 6'2" tall and weighed 145 pounds. He kept his brown hair short. Later in life, his hair grew to collar length or longer and he grew a mustache. In 1961, Jeanette was sixteen years old. She was heavy for her age. Townspeople recall that Barbara was the prettiest of the Hitzfelder girls. She was thirteen years old in 1961.

Junior was quiet and kept to himself. He did not have many

friends. His few friends either felt sorry for him or associated with him because he could get away with mischief. Everyone was aware that Sheriff Charlie would always help Junior out of trouble. Later in life, interviews of his teenage friends indicated they believed Junior was either homosexual or bisexual. Junior had no real friends.

Sheriff Charlie was believed to be violent, stern, and demanding. He often punished his son to keep him in line. Junior grew up fearing his father, spending a substantial amount of time at his grandparents' home in La Coste, fifteen miles east of Hondo, near the small community of Castroville. The sheriff's daughters, Jeanette and Barbara, were treated significantly better than Charlie Jr. was by their father. Some say this was because Charlie never wanted a son. Charlie's dislike for boys could be traced to his own childhood when he was required to care for his smaller brothers. This led to a lifetime of hatred of Junior. Charlie's intense hostility toward his son was occasionally observed in public.

As Junior grew, it was apparent he would never live up to his father's expectations. No matter how hard junior tried to please his father, he only seemed to disappoint him. Junior learned that if he wanted his father's attention, he needed to act out. Junior was a constant problem for the sheriff, always in some kind of trouble.

Law enforcement officers in Medina County knew junior, not only because he was Charlie's son, but also because they had to deal with Junior's misdeeds. As a teenager, Junior abused alcohol. Later in life, he became a severe alcoholic. Throughout his life, Charlie was always able to get his son out of trouble, thereby protecting his political legacy. Junior, often truant from school, had poor grades. Junior attended public school in Hondo. After three years at Hondo High School his troubles with teachers came to a head. The school district had enough of junior's antics. He had offended most of the staff and all of his fellow students. The high school was desperate to do something with Junior. The school administrators went to the sheriff and told him they had done all they could and would no longer deal with junior. They told the sheriff that junior was a very smart young man and capable of being a likeable and compassionate person.

Junior continued to act up, and to the school's surprise, Charlie agreed to transfer his son to a small continuation school in D'Hanis, a few miles south of town. Junior would never graduate from either school.

Junior was not good at sports to the sheriff's great disappointment, never trying out for any of the school's teams. Junior was not big enough or fast enough to play football, which was a huge disappointment to his father. Besides his lack of interest in sports, junior showed even less interest in having a career.

Junior seemed happy working menial jobs. He never expressed a desire to learn a trade until after he was in the U.S. Navy. In 1963, Junior told officials that he hoped to go into law enforcement like his father, but this only came after a brush with the law.

Jeanette and Barbara, Junior's sisters were seldom seen on dates with boys. This was apparently their father's doing. Charlie told his daughters he was protecting them from the bad people in the world. The daughters must have known Charlie only wanted to control them, as dating offered them a chance for some freedom. Charlie always needed be in control. The sisters had good relationships with their mother, Iona, who also wanted to rule the roost.

Iona often stepped in to protect her daughters from their father's anger, which was usually verbal. Sheriff Charlie was mostly good to the girls, but was suspected of abusing junior psychologically. While the sheriff abused Iona verbally, she was seen slapping Charlie in the face as they drove through town. Eyewitnesses also reported seeing Charlie hitting Iona in town.

Iona's brother was a highway patrolman in a nearby county. By 1961, Iona had been around law enforcement officers for over a decade. Charlie made her a deputy sheriff, so she carried a 38-caliber pistol in her purse. Iona sometimes worked the radio at the sheriff's office. For Iona, being the sheriff's wife was the next best thing to being sheriff. Iona demanded respect, like the sheriff, which caused townspeople to fear her. Merchants knew better than to cross Iona. Her affairs with a deputy and a local merchant were well known around town.

People wondered if Iona was a battered wife. Mary Ruth Cadenhead, Junior's first wife reports that she was not abused. Others disagreed. Battered women in the 1940 and 1950s rarely had the courage to leave an abusive man. In the Hitzfelder relationship, many believed this was a relationship both wanted. Both enjoyed the political power involved in being the sheriff. Iona would never be sheriff, so being the sheriff's wife and deputy was the next best thing. It was a perfect combination. As for their children, they hoped to grow up and leave Hondo. It would be safe to say that all three of the Hitzfelder children grew up isolated from certain aspects of growing up.

The Hitzfelder marriage may have been launched by love, but stayed afloat by convenience. Iona knew she would never run for sheriff against her husband, so being his wife and a deputy was the next best thing. While Charlie and Iona enjoyed their positions of authority and power in the community, their children looked forward to leaving Hondo. Their isolated lives robbed them of certain aspects of growing up.

As a teenager, Junior held several jobs, most only lasting a few months. These jobs were secured by his father. Junior worked for Alamo Aviation at the San Antonio Airport for four months. He also worked at Jenkins Phillips 66 Service Station, Lutz's Sinclair Station, and Tommy's Gulf Station for three months each.

His longest-running job was at the Raye Theater in Hondo. This was a very desirable job for a teenager, allowing him to see movies and impress girls. Junior began working at the Raye Theater when he was eleven and continued on until fifteen. Junior met many young girls while working at the theater.

In 1959, when Junior was seventeen, he met a fourteen-year-old girl from nearby Devine, twenty miles east of Hondo in Medina County. Mary Ruth Cadenhead was a beautiful child, who grew into an attractive woman. At 5'3" tall, she was a short, slender woman with medium-dark well-groomed hair. Junior's friends reported that he was only interested in having sex with Mary Ruth in the back seat of his 1956 Chevrolet. Charlie disapproved of their relationship. Mary's mother, a schoolteacher in Devine, also disapproved of Junior and Mary Ruth's affair. Mary Ruth's father despised Junior. Early on, Sheriff Charlie demanded that Junior end the relationship. Junior told his father that he would stop seeing Mary Ruth, but continued to drive to Devine for secret late night liaisons. In spite of her disdain for Charlie, Mary Ruth's mother would help her daughter sneak her out of the house to meet him.

Mary Ruth said that at 14, she was young and naïve. She said she was not accustomed to the ways of the world yet. Junior was a smooth talker and convinced Mary Ruth that he loved her. In October 1960, junior was picked up by Sheriff's Deputy Verner Muennink for being a minor in possession of alcohol. Since the deputy was having an affair with Junior's mother, he protected junior, as he had done several times in the past. Iona and Verner kept many of junior's antics hidden from the sheriff. Iona doted over her son, and kept Junior's misdeeds a secret from the sheriff whenever she could.

Mary Ruth learned that she was pregnant in October 1960. She wanted to keep the baby, while her parents wanted her to get an abortion. In the 60s if you got pregnant, you either got married or had an abortion. Mary Ruth insisted on keeping the baby, much to the disappointment of her parents. She telephoned Junior asking him to come to her house in Devine. She told him that she had important news. When Junior got to the house, Mary Ruth and her mother told Junior that he was going to be a father. Junior turned white and said he was not ready to have a child. Mary Ruth's father laid out the options for Junior. Junior either married Mary Ruth, or face being arrested for having sex with a minor. Junior was more afraid of what his father would say, than of being arrested. Junior went to his mother and shared the news.

Iona told the sheriff that Junior had gotten Mary Ruth pregnant. This was the final straw for the sheriff, who knew that if Junior did not wed Mary Ruth, his chances for reelection would be slim. A sheriff traditionally stands for family values. A scandal such as this would crush Charlie's chances for reelection. The sheriff delivered his ultimatum to Junior: he must marry Mary Ruth. He also told Junior that he would have to join the Navy as a means to support his family. Junior was terrified, but soon realized this may be his ticket out of Hondo.

As a backup plan, Iona arranged for a doctor to abort Mary Ruth's baby. Before Mary Ruth and Iona left for San Antonio Mary Ruth called Junior and told him she was going to have the abortion that afternoon. Junior was still unsure of what to do, so Mary Ruth gave him the doctor's telephone number. Later that day, while Iona and Mary Ruth were waiting to see the doctor, Junior called and asked to speak to her. Junior told her that he had decided to get married. This was good news for Mary Ruth, as she wanted to keep the baby.

Plans were made for Mary Ruth and Charlie to marry before his enlistment date. Iona's cousin arranged a ceremony with a minister in San Antonio. Later that week, Junior went to San Antonio and enlisted in the Navy. He was told to report to basic training in San Diego on October 26, 1960.

Unknown to Mary Ruth, Junior continued to see another very young girl, Claudette Carolyn Covey, after his marriage. Carolyn was thirteen when Junior met her at the Raye Theater, where Junior worked as an usher. Carolyn was from a poor family, living on the wrong side of the tracks. The wrong side of the tracks is the northern portion of Hondo. The area is located just north of US 90 and runs parallel with the Southern Pacific Railroad tracks. This was an area of mostly poorer families. Carolyn's father worked seven days a week as a cedar chopper. Carolyn was a pretty, petite young girl at 5'3" tall and 115 pounds. She had brunette hair and was very young and vulnerable.

Carolyn was the second oldest of six daughters. The family shared a small two-bedroom house on the poor side of town. All of the girls shared beds. Carolyn was thought to be promiscuous by some of the townsfolk. This was probably due to her likeable personality and willingness to hitchhike around town. Young girls rarely hitchhiked in 1961. The boys in town were attracted to Carolyn for her good looks and pleasant personality. She was easygoing and a free spirit. Junior was believed to be supplying Carolyn with beer and pocket change. Junior's motives were clear: he was interested in having sex with Carolyn. After a few dates,

Junior stole Carolyn's innocence. They continued to see one another in spite of Junior's marriage to Mary Ruth.

Mary Ruth believed Charlie was her one and only love. She did not know about Carolyn, who lived in Devine was twenty miles from Hondo. Neither girl was old enough to drive, so Junior was able to keep each from finding out about the other. Many in town believed that Junior fell in love with Carolyn. Her perky, smiling personality was easy to like. Even though he loved Carolyn, Junior knew better than to consider leaving Mary Ruth for her. His reluctance wasn't her age, but her social status. She was poor and did not meet the Hitzfelder family standards. Junior decided to hide this relationship from his father. He feared his father would never approve and put a stop to it.

As Junior was getting ready for the Navy, he told Carolyn he would not be seeing her as often as he had. Their relationship was supposed to be a secret, but Carolyn's sisters knew about their romance. Carolyn's mother and father never knew that Carolyn and Junior were romantically involved. Junior visited the Covey house on many occasions, but Mr. and Mrs. Covey thought Junior and Carolyn were only friends.

Word about Junior's affair with Carolyn had gotten back to the sheriff. He knew Carolyn from her hitchhiking and had seen her around town with some older local boys. Carolyn was not up to his standards. The sheriff looked down on anyone who lived on the wrong side of the tracks, regardless of what kind of person they were. If you had the misfortune to live on the poor side of town, you were trash to Sheriff Charlie. Twenty years later, Carolyn's sisters revealed that the sheriff had confronted Carolyn on at least three occasions, threatening her and suggesting it would be suicidal if she continued dating his son. After warning Carolyn, the sheriff told Iona that Junior was seeing a girl from the other side of the tracks. Iona was devastated. She wondered why Junior would make the family look bad by being seen with a girl like Carolyn Covey. Sheriff Charlie and Iona confronted Junior about Carolyn. They told Junior that they would not stand for such a romance. Junior, fearful of the potential consequences, told his parents that he would stop seeing Carolyn. But he would continue seeing

Carolyn behind his parents' backs.

After his parents' warning, Junior would park his car out of sight behind the Covey house when visiting Carolyn. The sheriff and his deputies could no longer see Charlie's car when he would visit. Charlie continued both affairs until he had to leave for the Navy.

TWO
In The Navy

Junior attended basic training at the North Island Training Facility in San Diego, successfully completing his eight-week boot camp.

As Christmas 1960 approached, Junior received leave. He flew to San Antonio, where Mary Ruth and her mother picked him up. Mary Ruth was three months pregnant. Mary Ruth's mother drove Junior to Hondo to pick up his 1956 Chevrolet. Upon arriving in Hondo, Junior told Mary Ruth that he needed to "take care of some things" and then would drive to Devine. Junior was dropped off at his parents' home and found that Iona was out shopping and Charlie was at the courthouse. He went inside the house, found the keys to his car, cranked up the motor, and off he went. Junior did not bother to tell his parents he was in town. He immediately headed over to see Carolyn. Junior and Carolyn took off for several hours. Later, Junior brought Carolyn home. It was late afternoon, and as Junior was driving through town, someone recognized him. They called the sheriff and asked how long Junior had been home. Charlie was outraged that Junior did not bother to tell him he was back in town.

Charlie left the courthouse and got in his sheriff's car. He drove through town looking for Junior. He was going to lay down the law to Junior. By now, Junior had dropped off Carolyn to meet with Melvin Pack. They bought some beer and were sitting in Junior's car at Tommy's Gulf Station.

The sheriff drove through town at high speeds. He was mad as hell. He found Junior and Melvin in the parking lot of Tommy's Gulf station. As Charlie drove into the parking lot of the station, he squealed his car to an abrupt stop. It was easy to see he was furious.

Junior and Melvin were standing in the parking lot talking. Melvin was a large boy, standing 5'10" tall and weighing over 200 pounds. He always wore glasses. Melvin saw the sheriff's car sliding to a stop. Junior was standing near his car. Sheriff Charlie got out of his car and screamed to Melvin, to go home. Melvin never said a word and he walked away from the station without wasting anytime. In a booming voice, Charlie demanded that junior to follow him home. The sheriff followed closely behind Junior to make sure he did not stray. When they got home, Iona had also just arrived. Her presence probably saved Junior from a beating. Iona was happy to see her son, but mad as hell when she found out that Junior had not spent much time with Mary Ruth before running off with his friends. Charlie wanted to punish him for his irresponsible behavior, screaming that he was going to teach him a lesson. Iona interrupted and told Charlie to deal with it later. She wanted make sure that Junior first dealt with his wife and unborn child. Charlie thought for a minute and reluctantly agreed to Iona's wishes. She demanded that Junior drive to Devine to be with Mary Ruth. The reunion at the Cadenhead house was not a joyful experience. Mary Ruth's dad was upset that Junior had been away for several hours, leaving Mary Ruth alone. He hated Junior. Mary Ruth was so upset she refused to come out of her room. Mary Ruth's mother insisted that she come out and sit with Junior. She came out of her room, but only for a few minutes.

Junior sensing the tension in the air decided it would be better for all if he returned the next day. He left the Cadenhead house and drove home. After returning home so quickly, Charlie and Iona demanded to know why the reunion was so short. He explained that Mary Ruth was upset with him for his behavior. The sheriff demanded that Junior turn over the keys to his car. Iona intervened, reminding her husband that their son would need transportation while on leave from the Navy. Charlie reluctantly relented, but lectured Junior on how his actions could have brought discredit to his family. Early the next day, Junior drove to Mary Ruth's house. Mary Ruth was calmer and agreed to leave with him for a drive in the country. Junior did not ask his pregnant wife how she had been feeling. He offered no compassion or understanding for her hurt feelings. She felt bewildered and alone. According to Mary Ruth, Charlie Jr. spent most of his time with her over his Christmas leave. Others tell a different story. Junior was often seen driving through Hondo with Carolyn Covey. Mary Ruth's biggest fear was that Junior would leave her and she would have her baby all alone. Mary Ruth had no knowledge of his affair with Carolyn Covey.

On Christmas day, Junior spent most of the day with Mary Ruth. She remembered that he had not responded to her letters when he was in basic training. He never called her. Even tough, Mary Ruth purchased several Christmas gifts for Junior, taking time to package the gifts with pretty paper and ribbons. She gave the gifts to Junior, but he showed up empty handed. The Cadenhead family wanted the best for Mary Ruth and did say anything about Junior's thoughtlessness. Junior told Mary Ruth that after his training, he was thinking of bringing her to California to live with him. Mary Ruth was stunned. She did not want to live with Junior. She wanted to finish high school, but did not say anything about her own dreams and wishes. She did not express her apprehension about moving to California. Deep down inside she feared Junior and the sheriff. Charlie Jr. left the Cadenhead house after a few hours. He told Mary Ruth that he had to go visit his grandparents. Mary Ruth said she wanted to go with him. He lied to Mary Ruth and told her that he would be right back. After he left the Cadenhead home, no one spoke of his insensitivity. Mary Ruth was crushed emotionally and retreated to her room. She cried for hours. Later that day, Mary Ruth confided to her mother that she was devastated over Charlie's lack of caring.

Junior drove back to Hondo, straight to Carolyn's house. Still afraid of being caught by his parents, he parked his car in the backyard and entered through the back door. It was discovered years later that Junior carried in with him a bag with a wrapped Christmas present. Junior gave the present to Carolyn, spending only a few minutes at the Covey house. He took Carolyn for a drive in the county. Finding a secluded spot just outside of town, he offered her some beer he had picked up at one of the Ice

House's in town.

After indulging, Junior asked Carolyn to climb into the back seat of his car. She succumbed to Junior's advances. In jest, he thanked Carolyn for his Christmas present. After the passion, he asked Carolyn for her panties. She thought this strange and asked why. Junior replied that the panties would be his remembrance of the day. Carolyn told him that she would not do this. Junior became extremely agitated, but Carolyn calmed him. Carolyn smiled at Junior and told him that she loved him. He changed the subject. Charlie Jr. drove Carolyn home. Junior drove around Hondo until he found Melvin Pack. The two then drove around drinking beer. Just before sundown, he returned to Devine to be with Mary Ruth. As he walked into the house, his drinking was apparent. Mr. Cadenhead asked him where he had been all day. Junior responded by saying that he had spent the day with his family. Mr. Cadenhead was suspicious but did not say anything. After a few hours, Junior said he needed to go home to spend the rest of the day with his mother. He drove back to Hondo for the night.

The next morning, Junior decided to tell his mother not of his love for Mary Ruth but of his love for Carolyn. He told his mother that he never really loved Mary Ruth. He told his mother that Carolyn was the girl he wanted to be with. Iona asked if Carolyn was the girl from poor side of town. Junior told his mother that Carolyn was poor but quickly added it did not make a difference to him. Iona could not contain her displeasure and began screaming at him. She reminded him of the family's status in town. She asked him why he wanted to destroy all his father had worked for. She demanded that the relationship with Carolyn end. Junior once again professed his love for Carolyn. Iona was not at all concerned with what Junior wanted. She discounted his feelings and reminded him that his father was an important and powerful man. She said that a relationship like this could cause the family embarrassment. Iona once again demanded that Junior stop seeing Carolyn. Junior stood his ground and told his mother that he wanted a divorce from Mary Ruth, freeing him to marry Carolyn. Iona never expected her children to bring discredit on the family. Now furious, she got on the phone and called Charlie. Iona told the Sheriff that his son wanted to divorce Mary Ruth, so he could continue to see a young girl from the wrong side of the tracks. Charlie was outraged and said he would be home in a minute. The courthouse was only five minutes away.

While waiting for his father, Junior realized the mess he was in and begged his mother to understand his love for Carolyn. Junior expressed his well-founded fear that Sheriff Charlie might take matters into his own hands. Iona searched for a compromise. She thought it was best for now to help her son get out of the mess he was in with Charlie. Iona decided that she would help him—but at a price. She told Junior not to see Carolyn the remainder of his leave. Junior agreed and said he would spend all of his time with Mary Ruth. Minutes later, the sheriff arrived home. He was furious. When he entered the front room, Iona and Junior were sitting on the couch. Charlie immediately lashed out at his son. He ranted and raved about the affair. He told his son that Carolyn was just no good. He said Junior's relationship with Carolyn was going to hurt his chances for reelection. Charlie continued his rant, demanding Junior go with him to the Covey house and breakup with Carolyn. Junior for the first time in his life refused the sheriff's request. Realizing that Charlie was very serious, and could do anything, he thought of a compromise. Junior told his father that he would return to San Diego ahead of his scheduled return on January 8, 1961. Charlie warned his son that no one would interfere with him keeping his job as sheriff and if he saw Carolyn again, he would regret it. He told his son that people have a way of ending up dead in Medina County for as little as $50. He reminded his son of what he told him when he was very young, "Two bullets to the back of anyone's head gets the job done." Charlie finished by saying that if he disobeyed him, someone would not live to regret it.

It was December 29, 1960. Charlie Jr. for the most part kept his word to his father. He was in Devine most of the time with Mary Ruth. When he could, Junior would sneak away to meeting with Carolyn. On the day Charlie Jr. left for San Diego, Iona reminded her son that she knew about Carolyn. She cautioned him that he would be live to regret going back on his word. Iona and Mary Ruth drove Charlie Jr. to the San Antonio Airport in the 1956 Chevrolet, which was Junior's pride and joy.

THREE
The Wrong Way Out

BART BUTLER, TONY RAMEY

SHE FOUND OUT THE WORLD AIN'T FLAT
ON THE OTHER SIDE OF THE RAILROAD TRACKS
SO SHE CROSSED A LINE THAT YOUNG GIRLS JUST DON'T CROSS
AND SHE LEARNED WHAT TO COMPROMISE
HOW TO TALK TO MEN WITH THOSE LYIN' EYES
'TIL ONE DAY HER INNOCENCE WAS LOST

ON A BACKROAD OFF THE HIGHWAY, IN A BACK SEAT OF A CAR
SHE GIVES HERSELF AWAY TO A COLD DECEITFUL HEART

(CHORUS)
SHE WAS LOOKIN' FOR THE WRONG WAY OUT
OF A SOUTHWEST TEXAS TOWN
SHE WAS GOIN' TOO FAR AND NOW
IT'S COMIN' BACK AROUND
THERE'S A RED MOON ARISIN'
AND A STAR THAT SHE WISHED UPON IS GONE BEHIND A CLOUD
SHE WAS LOOKIN' FOR THE WRONG WAY OUT

SOMEWHERE A SMOKIN' GUN
AND THE TRUTH ABOUT A SHERIFF'S SON
IS BURIED WITH A YOUNG GIRLS UNBORN CHILD
THE DEVILS IN POWER AND POLITICS
AND HE FIXES THINGS THAT CAN'T BE FIXED
AND THE LONG ARM OF THE LAW CAN REACH FOR MILES

AND THERE LAY JULIE'S BABIES IN A FIELD ALL ALONE
AND A PAST THAT'S DARK AND HAZY WITH THE WORDS CARVED OUT IN STONE

(REPEAT CHORUS)

(TAG)
SHE FOUND OUT THE WORLD AIN'T FLAT
ON THE OTHER SIDE OF THE RAILROAD TRACKS
SO SHE CROSSED A LINE THAT YOUNG GIRLS JUST DON'T CROSS

"She Was Looking For The Wrong Way Out"

Valentine's Day, February 14, 1961, was a normal day in Hondo. Carolyn Covey attended her classes at Hondo High School. After school, Carolyn and her sisters, Barbara, twelve, and Alice, sixteen, were waiting at home for two local boys. Adolph "Dewey" Saathoff and Melvin Pack were supposed to stop by. Dewey, who was dating Alice Covey, was short in stature with a round face. He looked Hispanic and was easily recognized by everyone in town due to his physical characteristics. Alice and Dewey were very close, and later married. Carolyn asked Dewey to drive her and her sisters to Buck's Drive Inn. Carolyn wanted to purchase binder paper and glue for her scrapbook. She wanted to paste in the Valentine cards she had received at school that day. Dewey agreed, and they all got into his car and drove to the Ice House, parking out front. The girls went inside and Carolyn purchased the paper and glue.

According to Alice and Dewey, after leaving the Ice House they all drove down Avenue M. Carolyn told Dewey she wanted to get out of the car. Dewey stopped the car on Avenue M near the Lutheran Church, not far from Carolyn's house. As Carolyn got out of the car, she told her sisters that she was going to walk up town again. Carolyn said she would be home in an hour or so. It was around 6:30 P.M. No one thought twice about Carolyn getting out of the car. Hondo was immune to big city crimes and serious issues. Forty-eight years later, Alice and Dewey continue to offer the same version of events on that night, the last time they saw Carolyn.

After Carolyn got out of Dewey's car, he continued down Avenue M and dropped off Alice and Barbara Covey at their house. When the girls went into the house, Mrs. Covey asked where Carolyn was. The sisters told their mother that Carolyn went back into town. Mrs. Covey was concerned that Carolyn was not with her sisters, but Carolyn's free spirit accounted for this kind of behavior. Carolyn often took off, returning a few hours later. Dewey and Melvin left the house, intending to go night road-hunting for deer. As they drove back down Avenue M, they passed the Lutheran Church and saw Carolyn walking toward town. Carolyn saw Dewey and Melvin as they passed, but didn't appear angry at them as she gave them a comical look.

After two hours passed, Julie Covey began to worry about Carolyn. She had a gut feeling something was wrong. Mrs. Covey was a stay-at-home mom. Her children were her life. Carolyn's father, Albert, was a tall, lanky man. His family was also everything to him. When he heard that Carolyn had not returned home, he too was frantic. He drove to the Sheriff's Department to report Carolyn missing. Albert Covey was told that the Sheriff's Department would do nothing about Carolyn's disappearance. The dispatcher told Albert that Carolyn had not been missing very long and would probably show up soon. He got into his car and drove over to Dewey's house. He learned that Dewey and Melvin did not know where Carolyn was. Albert Covey then drove to the Gulf station, arriving around 9:00 P.M. as Dennis Heyen was closing the station.

Dennis offered to help look for Carolyn. He had dated her on occasion, and was also concerned. In the past, he often helped Carolyn with her homework. Dennis closed up shop and drove to his boss's house and dropped off the night's receipts. He then found Dewey and Alice. The three drove around all night looking for Carolyn. They did not find Carolyn. As daybreak came, the Covey family was terrified. They knew something was wrong after spending a sleepless night wondering what had happened to her. That morning, Mr. Covey called the Sheriff's Department again and asked for help in finding Carolyn. The sheriff's dispatcher called Sheriff Charlie and told him of the Covey family's concerns. Sheriff Charlie soon called the Covey house, telling Mr. Covey that Carolyn had probably run off with someone and would be home soon. Charlie refused to organize a search for Carolyn. As the day came to an end, the Covey family became increasingly desperate.

After two days, there had been no word on Carolyn's whereabouts, so the family asked around town for help in organizing a search party. Concerned townsfolk gathered the following day, February 16, to devise a search plan. Only a few townspeople showed up. One of the volunteers told Mr. Covey that Sheriff Charlie told townspeople not to participate in the search, because he believed "Carolyn had just run off." He cautioned them about interfering with sheriff business. The people in town, while concerned about Carolyn's disappearance, knew better than to cross Sheriff Charlie. For the next two days, the Covey family and a few friends searched tirelessly for Carolyn, looking in open fields and abandoned buildings. They drove up and down county roads for miles and miles. No sign of Carolyn was found. Four days after her disappearance, the sheriff finally sent out a teletype to local law enforcement, asking them to be on the lookout for a runaway girl from Hondo.

Word about Carolyn's disappearance eventually made it to the San Antonio newspapers. In the 1960s, reports of missing or abducted children were rare. Members of the press made several calls to the Sheriff's Department. Sheriff Charlie fielded the calls. He reported that he was on top of Carolyn's disappearance from the very beginning. Sheriff Charlie told the press that he and his men had been tirelessly looking for any signs of Carolyn Covey. Because of the calls from the press, Charlie finally organized a search for Carolyn and headed it himself. Charlie finally asked for help from the townsfolk. About thirty people answered the call. They searched in and around Hondo for two days. Sheriff Charlie, bowing to pressure from the press, asked for help from the Texas Highway Patrol. The sheriff sent a request to the Texas Department of Public Safety (DPS), asking them to put Carolyn's photo in the weekly DPS bulletin distributed to law enforcement agencies throughout the state.

One of Charlie's deputies, Harry Raby, drove twenty miles to the Campsey house in Devine. Donald "Butch" Campsey sometimes worked for Raby on his ranch. Harry knew that the Campsey boys had received a set of walkie-talkies for Christmas. The deputy asked to borrow the walkie-talkies to help in the search. Butch eagerly agreed. Butch Campsey would one day be elected sheriff, winning the 1976 election in Medina County.

Days of searching by the Covey family were fruitless. No one found any sign of Carolyn. As months went by, Charlie would continue to answer reporters' questions, telling them he had leads into Carolyn's disappearance. He said he had suspicions as to what happened to Carolyn, telling the press that he was on top of all possibilities concerning her whereabouts.

Carolyn's disappearance launched a nine-month campaign with Charlie routinely telling the press he was interviewing and investigating potential suspects. Over the next few weeks, the sheriff asked the Texas Rangers to conduct polygraph tests of various suspects. Carolyn's father was among them. DPS examiner, J. Ray Sanders, concluded that Mr. Covey knew nothing about Carolyn's disappearance. The examiner for unknown reasons conveyed in his written report that there were questionable responses coming from Mr. Covey. For unknown reasons the examiner was concerned that Mr. Covey may have had sexual relations with Carolyn. The relevance of this questioning had little to do with Carolyn's disappearance. Polygraphs were administered to over twenty people. It seemed that almost anyone who knew Carolyn was subjected to a polygraph test. But even then, some people in town who had bad reputations were not asked to take a polygraph. Some surmised Charlie was just trying to look like he was on top of the case. In addition to conducting polygraph tests on townspeople, Charlie had other suspects in a five-state area tested. Newspaper accounts at the time reported that Charlie had been in Colorado, El Paso, Mexico, and East Texas investigating potential suspects. Whenever Charlie learned that a law enforcement agency had locked up a kidnapping suspect, he would travel there to question the man. While this satisfied some, the townspeople knew better. Many thought Charlie was diverting the investigation. In time, the press became suspicious, doubtful that Charlie was putting much effort into Carolyn Covey's disappearance. These suspicions began to circulate as far away as San Antonio. Charlie was forced to tell a reporter with the *San Antonio Express* and News the following: *Contrary to belief by some around here in Hondo, my deputies and I have been working any and all leads from day one of this girl's disappearance*. Charlie told the press that he had solid leads and expected to make an announcement soon. This "lead" was never again mentioned to the press.

After the initial reports of Carolyn's disappearance, two legendary Texas Rangers became involved in the case. Captain Alfred Y. Allee, the head ranger of Company E in Uvalde and Ranger Levy Duncan, stationed in Medina County, assisted Sheriff Charlie. Captain Allee was a legend throughout Texas since the early 1950s. Allee was smaller in stature than most Texas Rangers at just under six feet. He weighed approximately 190 pounds. His hair began to gray in 1961. Ranger Duncan was the stereotypical Texas Ranger: tall and well built. Both rangers wore long-sleeve white shirts, custom-fitted western slacks, cowboy boots, and the ever-present Stetson hat - felt in the winter and straw in the summer. Ranger Duncan was responsible for the four counties in San Antonio area, including Medina County. He was the man who got the call when the sheriff needed help.

A few weeks into Carolyn's disappearance, a local businessman reported a potential lead to the Texas Rangers. Ranger Captain Allee and Ranger Levy Duncan were in town investigating Carolyn's disappearance. It was common for rangers to be involved in disappearances and abductions. The lead came from Joe Fohn who operated White's Auto Store. Joe was small in stature and hard-working. Joe sold auto parts and accessories such as seat covers. The rangers were seeking eyewitnesses when they entered White's Auto. Joe approached the rangers and said he had some information about Carolyn Covey's disappearance.

Joe had been afraid to provide Sheriff Charlie with his information. The day Carolyn Covey went missing, he remembered seeing Charlie Jr. driving around town. Joe was positive it was he, recognizing his 1956 Chevrolet. Joe said he was close enough to see the car's new seat covers, which Charlie Jr. had purchased from him months before. The seat covers stood out in Joe's mind because Charlie Jr. had charged the seat covers and never paid for them. Joe did not know if the information was important, but he told the rangers that people around town believed Junior was seeing Carolyn Covey. He kept this from the sheriff, fearful of how the sheriff might take it. The rangers thanked Joe for the information and assured him that they would keep it in confidence. A few hours later, the rangers went to the county courthouse. Captain Allee walked into Charlie's office and told him what Joe Fohn had said about his son. Sheriff Charlie was taken aback at first, but told Captain Allee that this information was not credible. He told Captain Allee that Charlie Jr. was in San Diego that day, adding he could verify this. The rangers believed Charlie and did not press the sheriff any further on the subject. The next day, after the rangers left town, Charlie drove over to White's Auto. He stormed inside the store and found Joe Fohn in the back room. Charlie cornered Joe, who could see that Charlie was furious. Charlie's eyes pierced right through Joe's soul. He grabbed Joe around his shirt collar and declared that people who know too much have a way of ending up dead or missing in his county.

This was all Charlie had to say. He turned and walked out of the store. Joe was terrified. He realized that he should have kept his mouth shut. He was now facing his worst nightmare - an angry, powerful sheriff, who now had reason to silence him. Joe went home that night and could not sleep.

The next few days came and went before Charlie decided that a second visit to the store was in order. As before, Charlie took Joe aside and lectured him about keeping quiet. Charlie told him that people could be killed around there for as little as fifty bucks. Joe became a nervous wreck, constantly looking over his shoulder. Loud noises sent him into a panic. On the following Friday night, Joe was driving alone from Hondo to San Antonio down a dark county road. There were few other cars on the road. Joe looked into his rearview mirror and saw the headlights of a fast approaching car. The speeding car quickly caught up to Joe's car. The mysterious driver was continuously flashing the high beams and honking his horn. Joe was scared as hell. He slowed down, hoping the car would pass. It did not. The driver inched closer to Joe's car, nearly touching Joe's rear bumper. Suddenly the driver accelerated, and began striking Joe's rear bumper. After the third strike, Joe lost control of his car and went into a spin, sliding off the road into a ditch. The other car sped off.

Joe was unhurt but frightened beyond belief. Joe Fohn said he never saw the driver or what kind of car ran him off the road. One thing was clear, Joe never repeated the story he told Ranger Evans until Sheriff Charlie was voted out office in 1976. Joe finally told his story to newly elected Sheriff Butch Campsey.

FOUR
And There Lies Someone's Babies In a Field All Alone

Halloween Day, October 31, 1961, began as a normal day for Mrs. Scotty Bailey on her small cattle ranch just outside of Yancey, Texas. The Bailey farm was located on FM 462, about halfway between Hondo and Yancey, a distance of about 8 miles. Mrs. Bailey was a middle-aged woman who once worked as a teacher and now worked part time at a local feed store. Mrs. Bailey and her husband raised twenty to thirty head of cattle for food and extra money. The Bailey ranch was around 20 acres, but that didn't include a small pasture they leased adjacent to their property, which is located on Farm to Market 462 and intersects County Road 545. Live Oak Creek runs along FM 462 and under the pavement onto the Bailey farm. Scotty, as Mrs. Bailey was known and her husband were out walking their property, gathering cows that had strayed from the herd. Scotty was walking near Live Oak Creek, which was dry much of the year.

Scotty was about 400 yards south of their home when she noticed an object on the ground near some mesquite brush. It appeared to be the bone of a deer. Scotty kicked the large bone and was horrified to see it was actually a human skull. She screamed and her husband ran over to her. The two bent to the ground and stared at the skull. Scotty ran into the house and called the Sheriff's Department.

Mr. Bailey waited for the sheriff to arrive and looked around the area. He saw numerous bones in the adjacent mesquite brush, including leg bones, a pelvis, and vertebrae. Found near the bones was a pair of red-colored woman's shorts.

After calling the Sheriff's Department, Scotty returned to the creek bed. Her husband showed her the bones he had found. The two stood there silently, stunned at their find. Scotty later said they waited for nearly one hour before a Sheriff's Deputy arrived at the ranch. As they waited, the Baileys wondered if they had located the bones of the girl who went missing from Hondo.

When the first deputy arrived near the Bailey Ranch on FM 462, Scotty walked to the fence near CR 545, which intersects FM 462. The fence line on CR 545 was only thirty-one steps from where the bones were found. She walked to the fence and climbed over it, meeting the deputy and telling him of their terrible find. The deputy wondered out loud if this was the Covey girl as he made his way over to the bones. He stood there for a minute and then returned to his car. He asked to use the Bailey's telephone. Scotty and the deputy drove up to the Bailey house. She opened the door and pointed to her telephone. Scotty said the deputy was talking to Sheriff Charlie, indicating his belief that the Covey girl's body may have been found. The Sheriff told the deputy to stay put and wait for his arrival.

Over the next hour, another deputy arrived and both men walked to the crime scene The deputies looked at the various human bones, which were confined to an area of five to ten feet. There was no sign of a recent grave, making it appear as though the body had been dumped.

The ground was hard as stone at the site. The back of the skull had two small bullet holes, consistent with a small caliber gun. It was also clear that this was a murder.

At about 3 P.M., the sheriff's unmarked car arrived at the Bailey ranch. Sheriff Charlie parked on FM 462, about twenty yards from his deputies. In the car with Sheriff Charlie was Carolyn's mother, Julie Covey. Ms. Covey held Sally, her seven-month-old daughter in her arms. The sheriff told Ms. Covey to wait in the car. She was terrified and confused as to what was going on. When she received a call from the sheriff's office, she had been told that Carolyn may have been found and nothing more. During the drive from Hondo to the Bailey ranch, Charlie refused to answer any of Mrs. Covey's questions. Charlie climbed over the fence and walked to the deputies, who had been standing vigil near the body's remains for over an hour. The deputies pointed out the various bones. Charlie took particular interest in the skull, bending over and picking up the skull. He said, "I guess this one isn't talking anymore." Charlie then placed the skull under the crook of his left arm and walked back towards his car. He climbed over the fence and approached Julie Covey, who was cradling her baby. Charlie opened the car door and dropped the skull into her arms. The sheriff asked if this was Carolyn. Mrs. Covey broke down. Her screams must have been heard for miles. She was hysterical, afraid to drop the skull, while wondering if this was her baby. Years later, Julie Covey recalled that she immediately felt her heart sink and she felt like dying. Julie continued to wail and cry. After a minute or so, Charlie took the skull from Mrs. Covey and walked away. As he walked from the car, Julie Covey realized that the sheriff was sending her a message, a message about his power and her impotence. Julie recalled the sheriff's threats to Carolyn. Charlie told a deputy to transfer Ms. Covey to the deputy's car and take her home. As the deputy drove Julie home, she continued to cry. She was sick to her stomach and felt like her world had come to an end. Julie Covey was sure the Sheriff Charlie had something to do with Carolyn's murder, but never spoke on the way home.

The Crime Scene Investigation
The Star That She Wished Upon is Behind a Cloud

In 1961, modern crime scene forensics was at least twenty-five years away. DNA had not yet been developed as a law enforcement tool. Blood evidence was largely restricted to blood typing or identifying blood as animal or human. Trace evidence, as it is called today, was limited to shoe prints, tire tracks, tool markings, and possibly fiber or thread analysis. The crime scene investigator was limited to black and white photography, fingerprints, shoe or tire prints, dental record identification, and eyewitness testimony. If a murderer dumped a victim in a remote area, it could be weeks or months before the body was found. If a dumped body was found quickly, there were limited ways to identify the victim, such as fingerprints. On occasion, a coroner could compare the deceased's teeth to dental charts of known missing people. If there was no clothing or identification on or near a decomposed body, the teeth were a detective's most important clue. Abnormality of bone structure or a healed broken bone also has helped in the identification process.

In the Southwest United States from the 1950s to the mid-1980s there were over 1,000 unidentified murder victims due to extreme decomposition and a lack of identification at the crime scene. Many of these victims were young girls accused of being promiscuous. These girls were rarely reported missing in a timely manner and few had dental charts to aid in identification.

She crossed a Line that Young Girls Don't Cross

The sheriff called in the Texas Rangers for help with the crime scene. Their work was limited, consisting of collecting Carolyn's bones and the red-colored shorts, and taking black and white photos. Since the rangers were involved, it was expected that an area grid search would be undertaken. There is no record of that work being conducted. It is not known what the rangers actually did at the crime scene. To this day, they refuse to share this information. Carolyn Covey's remains were taken to the Sheriff's Department in a cardboard box and not to a funeral home. Carolyn's bones were stored in a large box for twenty-three years, after which she was finally laid to rest. Carolyn was buried in the Devine Cemetery in 1983. She now rests next to her mother and father, who died years after Carolyn.

Sadly, Albert Covey and Julie Covey would go to their own graves never knowing the full story of what happened to Carolyn. A few days after Carolyn was found, the Texas Rangers arranged to have her skull X-rayed. Medical experts confirmed it was her skull based on dental records provided by the Coveys. After this examination, Carolyn's remains were placed back into the cardboard box, where they remained locked away in the sheriff's property room until 1977. In 1962, the Covey family asked the sheriff if they could bury Carolyn's remains. Sheriff Charlie smugly asked the Coveys if they wanted someone digging up Carolyn's remains at a later date. He told them he would keep her remains in his office. The Coveys were stunned, but had no choice other than compliance. In 1977, the new Medina County Sheriff, Donald Butch Campsey, found Carolyn's remains in the courthouse evidence room. He was shocked that Carolyn's remains had been in storage for sixteen years. Butch took custody of Carolyn's remains and kept her bones with him for seven years, either in the trunk of his car or at a special place set up in his home. Finally, in 1983, Carolyn was laid to rest at the request of her mother, twenty-three years after her death. Sheriff Campsey and a fellow lawman, Chief Probation Officer Frank Perkins, spent the day with the Coveys and attended Carolyn's funeral.

Make An Arrest—Please The Press

In late 1961, after Carolyn's body was identified, Sheriff Charlie let it be known that he would personally solve Carolyn's murder. He decided to make an arrest and targeted Dennis Heyen as a suspect. He harassed and badgered Dennis almost daily for months. The sheriff would drive to the service station were Dennis worked and threatened to handcuff him, take him into the woods, and kill him, among other threats. The sheriff knew that Dennis Heyen had been romantically involved with Carolyn. After months of harassment, Dennis decided to leave town, taking a job in the west Texas oilfields. Charlie located Dennis and drove to west Texas, where he met Dennis at the Texas Highway Patrol office in Midland. He had been arrested by a highway patrolman. Dennis was interrogated at the Department of Public Safety office for two-and-one-half days. He was never charged with the murder of Carolyn. The full details of Dennis Heyen's arrest will be explored later.

Who Could Have Done This?

After Claudette Carolyn Covey's remains were found, townsfolk wondered who could have committed this terrible crime. The murder shocked the community. Before now, small towns like Hondo were supposed to be immune from such violent acts. Rumors circulated about whom could have been involved in Carolyn's disappearance and murder. The most repeated rumor then, and today, is that Charlie Junior committed this heinous act. Several people knew of Junior's relationship with Carolyn Covey. Many in town knew that Junior had few friends. Some even believed Junior was gay or some kind of pervert. All the rumors about Junior were whispered softly, as no one wanted to be targeted by Sheriff Charlie. Junior was in the Navy now, and this stopped some folks from passing the rumors along. In 1961, 1979, and again in 2009, Dennis Heyen reported seeing Charles Hitzfelder Jr. and Carolyn Covey together at the gas station where he was working on the night of February 13, 1961.

The sheriff was rumored to have had some involvement in Carolyn's murder. The sheriff was reluctant to search for Carolyn when she first disappeared. After her disappearance, he did not want townsfolk taking part in search parties. He wanted folks to mind their own business.

In 1979, Barbara Covey, Carolyn's sister, told Butch Campsey that Sheriff Hitzfelder accosted Carolyn on several occasions. The sheriff told Carolyn that he did not want her seeing his son because she was "no good." The sheriff threatened her, suggesting she could end up missing, or worse, never come home.

There was talk that Carolyn's involvement with Junior may have sent Sheriff Charlie over the edge. Carolyn was rumored to be pregnant with Charlie's baby. In 2009, Dennis Heyen said that Carolyn told him the sheriff had warned her to stop seeing his son. Rumors involving Sheriff Charlie or his son were never discussed in public, but only mentioned discreetly when the sheriff was not around.

People in town suspected Iona Hitzfelder might have been involved in Carolyn's death. Iona would never allow Junior to have a public relationship with Carolyn because of her social status. If Junior had gotten Carolyn pregnant, while married to Mary Ruth, Iona would have found this unacceptable. Iona was said to carry a 22 caliber or 38 caliber guns in her purse, carrying it everywhere she went. Carolyn was shot with a 22 caliber gun. She was known to have a terrible temper and never afraid to express her displeasure with someone. Most everyone knew Iona would do all she could to protect her family's status in town, as well as Charlie's position as sheriff.

There were many suspicions as to why Iona and Mary Ruth left town so suddenly around the time Carolyn disappeared. For the first time in 1981, a letter from the Hitzfelder family attorney to a Medina County judge finally put some light on when Iona and Mary Ruth left Hondo. The letter declared that in the early morning hours of February 14, 1961, Iona Hitzfelder and Mary Ruth Cadenhead drove from Hondo, Texas to San Diego, California in Junior's 1956 Chevrolet. The letter alleged that Iona and Mary Ruth left hours before Carolyn was last seen. However, this was not true. The stated purpose of this trip was to drive Mary Ruth, who was now six months pregnant, to be with Junior at the North Island training facility. Mary Ruth disputed the date herself in 2009. Mary Ruth said that she and Iona left Medina County the morning of February 15, after Carolyn's disappearance. She remembered the date because her father's birthday was February 14. Mary Ruth said that Iona and her drove alone to California. If Joe Fohn and Dennis Heyen were telling the truth, this puts Iona, Mary Ruth and Junior in Hondo the night of February 14, 1961—The night Carolyn disappeared. Mary Ruth said that they drove several hundred miles each day. At one of their stops, Iona called Sheriff Charlie. The sheriff told Iona that something big was going on in town and he could not talk. The next day, Iona called home again, and the sheriff told her that Carolyn Covey was missing. When they arrived in San Diego, Mary Ruth remembered Iona telling her son about Carolyn. Charlie Jr. blurted out that he used to date Carolyn. Mary Ruth insisted, forty-eight years later, that this was the only time Carolyn was spoken of during her stay in California.

Melvin Pack was a friend of Carolyn Covey and Dewey Saathoff. Melvin was riding with Dewey and the Covey girls the night Carolyn went missing. Most people in town immediately dismissed Melvin as a suspect, refusing to believe he could be involved in a murder. Melvin eventually left Hondo, moving to Grand Prairie, Texas. Melvin later worked as a police officer for the City of Grand Prairie. Melvin died of hardening of the arteries in 1977.

On the night Carolyn disappeared, Dewey and Melvin drove to the Covey house and picked up the Covey girls. Dewey drove Carolyn to Buck's Drive Inn to purchase notebook paper.

Her sisters Alice and Barbara accompanied.

On the way back home, Carolyn asked to get out of the car on Avenue M near the Lutheran Church and Dewey obliged. After dropping off Alice and Barbara Covey, Dewey passed back by the church and saw Carolyn walking toward town. Carolyn saw Dewey and Melvin as they passed. Dewey reported to Sheriff Charlie in 1961, and again in 1979 to Butch Campsey, that he and Melvin helped look for Carolyn that night. Dewey and Melvin were given a polygraph test and passed.

Orby Swatzell was Charlie's deputy in 1961. Orby Swatzell was asked to take a polygraph test after Carolyn's body was discovered. Orby's wife had came forward and reported that her husband was a sexual pervert. She reported graphic, deviant sexual behavior by her husband. The record reflects that Orby volunteered for a polygraph test. The DPS polygraph examiner determined that Orby was not involved in the Carolyn Covey murder.

Vernor Muennink worked as a deputy for Sheriff Charlie in the late 1950s and early in 1960. He was fired from his job after having sexual intercourse with a female inmate at the Medina County Jail. It was also learned that Vernor stopped a woman on FM 462 and propositioned her for sex. Vernor also owned land on FM 462 and had repaired some fencing on the same road. Carolyn was found just off this road. The DPS polygraph examiner determined that Vernor was not involved in the Carolyn Covey murder.

A local gas station proprietor and owner of Lutz's Sinclair Station, Charlie Lutz, was considered a suspect by some in town, but apparently not by the sheriff. For some reason, he was never subjected to a polygraph test.

Ervin Balzen was a twenty-one year old who lived on Avenue P about two blocks over from the Covey home. On the night of February 14, 1961, he admitted to walking down Avenue M, throwing rocks as he walked. One of those rocks broke a window at the old laundry across from the Lutheran Church. Ervin was arrested for vandalism the next night. Over two years later on October 28, 1963 he passed a polygraph test concerning the Covey murder.

Jerry Tondre was an eighteen-year-old boy from Pearsall, Texas. He admitted to seven dates with Carolyn Covey from October 1960 to November 27, 1960. He told police that he and Carolyn had done a little kissing, but he never had sexual intercourse. Jerry also said at the time of the polygraph that he thought Carolyn's reputation was spotless. He passed the polygraph test.

In 1961, Rodney James Freeman was sixteen. He told police that Dewey Saathoff had introduced him to Carolyn Covey. Rodney went out with Carolyn three or four times and admitted to having intercourse with her on one occasion. Rodney volunteered to take a polygraph test and was eliminated as a suspect after passing the test.

Rudy Garza was a 34-year-old janitor working at Lackland Air Force Base and living in Hondo. Someone reported to Sheriff Hitzfelder that Rudy was driving around town in his 1951 Mercury and had tried to pick up the Covey girls. Rudy denied this and offered to take a polygraph test. He passed the test.

Dewey Saathoff, Melvin Pack and Alice Covey, all who were the last to see Carolyn on February 14th, were eventually given polygraph tests by the Department of Public Safety. All three were said to have passed there polygraph tests.

The reader should know that in 1979, Sheriff Campsey learned both Dewey and Melvin were seen early in the morning of February 15, 1961 near where Carolyn's body was found. Two separate people came forward and reported passing the boys along FM 545 on their respective way to work. They recognized Melvin Pack and a boy thought to be Dewey—waving to both boys as they passed. The boys were "about 100 yards from the Yancey highway on FM 545". The boys were only 50 yards from where Carolyn's body was found 9 months later. The boys said on Valentine's night. 1961 they were headed out of town "road hunting" for deer. Sheriff Campsey said that deer are often located in this particular area of the county. The fact that the witnesses recalled seeing the boys' nine-months after the fact is interesting in itself. If this information were true, how did both boys pass polygraphs regarding their knowledge of Carolyn's death?

While writing this novel, I tried to interview Alice Covey-Saathoff, Carolyn's sister about the events of February 14, 1961. She refused to talk about the matter. Some other Covey family members were very helpful. I learned that Alice was warned by Sheriff Charlie in 1961, to "keep her mouth shut" while on a drive to Austin to take her polygraph test. I also learned that Alice Covey-Saathoff has recently said that she has information about her sisters' murder that will, "Blow your socks off".

There were other viable leads in Carolyn's case. On such lead came in 1981 when Butch Campsey was reviewing the case files when he ran across a notation that a traveling civil service worker named John Schulte recalled seeing a girl he felt was Carolyn on the night she disappeared. John's sister lived in Hondo, and he visited her often. Butch arranged a meeting with Schulte. He told Butch that on the night Carolyn disappeared he saw a girl he had often seen around town. The description of the girl was spot on, down to the clothing she was wearing that night. He gave her a ride to the Drive Inn on Highway 90. Schulte had very precise recollections of the night of February 14, 1961. Schulte's statements were consistent each and every time he related the story.

Schulte told sheriff Campsey that In 1961, he lived in San

Antonio. On Valentine's night in 1961 he was driving from San Antonio to Hondo. Before arriving in Hondo, he decided to visit his uncle in Quihi, just north of Hondo. After visiting his uncle, he drove into Hondo, intending to see his sister, who lived about three blocks from the Hitzfelder home. Around 6:15 P.M. Schulte was driving on Avenue M toward Hondo's main road, Highway 90. As he approached the Lutheran Church, he saw four or five "young people" standing in the parking lot near a black or blue colored "coupe" style car. As he approached the parked coupe a "skinny" teenage girl with dark hair stepped in front of his car motioning him to stop. The girl was fourteen or fifteen, wearing red shorts and a white blouse. Schulte had to stop abruptly, to avoid hitting the girl. She walked up to Schulte's car window and asked for a ride. The girl said she wanted to buy some notebook paper in town and needed a ride. Schulte said he was reluctant to help the girl because of her young age. He looked over at the group of teenagers and specifically remembers he also saw a short Hispanic male with a round face. Schulte exercised caution about giving a young girl a ride. He asked the girl why her friends could not drive her into town. She responded that her friends had "dates" and were busy. Schulte asked the girl to ask her friends if any of them wanted to ride along. The girl yelled to her friends, "You guys want to come along?" At the same time she appeared to be waving her friends off with hand gestures. Schulte reluctantly agreed to give her a ride. After getting into his car, she told Schulte she wanted a ride to the a Drive Inn on Highway 90. Schulte told the girl it was not safe for her to be out alone being so young. She replied that she was secretly meeting her boyfriend at 7 P.M. She said he was AWOL from the service and in town to take her back to California. The girl then intimated that she had a surprise for her boyfriend. When Schulte pressed her about her surprise, she said she just learned that she was pregnant. Schulte asked how the two were going to pay their bills and get by. She said she would get a job for awhile, and that her boyfriend was getting his service pay. She added only a few people knew about the rendezvous, because they were running off together. Her sisters back in the church parking lot agreed to cover for her with their mother until 9 P.M. This would give the couple a "two hour start" to get out of town. Schulte cautioned her that leaving like that could be a mistake. She said that they were in love and all would work out just fine.

Schulte continued onto Highway 90. The girl directed him to Hwy 90, to a beer joint she called "Buck's Drive Inn." As they arrived at the Ice House, the girl told Schulte not to worry about her safety. She said her boyfriend's father was the local sheriff, but did not know his son was in town, and the sheriff had no idea of their plans. The girl thanked Schulte for the ride and got out of the car. Schulte said he never saw the girl before that night and never saw her again.

Schulte added much more to his story. About one hour after dropping the young girl off, Schulte visited his sister Irene and his brother-in-law, Walter Grell. They lived at 2601 J Street. One of the families on the corner of Avenue I and 26th Street near Hondo High School were having a Valentine's Day party. Schulte said there were several cars parked at that particular intersection. He could hear party noises coming from within one of the houses. Schulte said that when you stood the side of his sister's house, the intersection was less than 100 feet away. He new this because, Schulte said he needed to use the bathroom that night, but his sister already occupied it. It was dark outside and Schulte could not wait. He went outside and urinated near an old wooden garage adjacent to his sister's house. Standing in the dark, Schulte could see the intersection. After relieving himself, Schulte lit a cigarette. While still outside, Schulte heard a loud "commotion" coming from the area of the intersection. He heard two men yelling as they stood by a green and white sedan. After nineteen years, Schulte still remembers what he overheard. An older man hollered, "You didn't even tell your mother you were in town." Then he heard, "I'm sorry daddy." There was a few seconds pause in the exchange. Next Schulte heard a car door open. Then a loud voice said, "You stupid son-of-a-bitch, look what you have done." A car door slammed and then there was silence. Schulte next heard a screen door open and close, and a few seconds later, he heard the screen door open and close again. Schulte heard noises similar to someone scuffling or fighting, and suddenly two distinct gunshots could be heard. Then there was silence. After a minute or so, he heard a man say, "As long as I'm sheriff, no one will hurt my son." A few minutes later, the car sped off into the night toward the "Yancey highway."

Schulte was terrified at what he heard and ran into his sister's house to tell her what happened. After listening to what her brother had to say, Irene warned him to "keep his mouth shut" about what he overheard. Schulte was reminded of the sheriff's infamous reputation. Irene and John Schulte did not want to get involved. Schulte agreed and did not report what he heard that night. They felt certain that something bad had happened. Even so, Schulte would be making a big mistake if he came forward. They both feared for their safety.

Nine months later, Carolyn Covey's body was found. People in town spoke of how Carolyn disappeared on Valentine's night. When her body was found in Yancey, the newspapers reported that Carolyn had been shot twice in the head. When John Schulte heard the news, he began to put things together. He knew what he overheard on Valentine's night was somehow connected to the girl's death. Schulte was too afraid to tell anyone outside his family what he knew and kept his secret for many years.

Thirteen years later in 1974 word that Schulte may have information about the Covey murder got back to Sheriff Hitzfelder. One afternoon in January or February 1974, Schulte was driving around Hondo. For no apparent reason, he was pulled over by Sheriff Hitzfelder. The sheriff was riding around town with his wife Iona at the time. Schulte said that he was put into the backseat of the car and "questioned" for about ten minutes by the sheriff about his knowledge of the Covey murder. Schulte said he told the sheriff he knew nothing about the Covey case and denied even being in town that night. Schulte said he was afraid that if he said anything, he could end up missing or dead. After the sheriff finished his questioning, Schulte was told to "get out of town," which he immediately did.

A few months later, Schulte thought things in town had quieted down. He decided to go to Hondo to visit his sister. While driving his car, he was again stopped by the sheriff. As before, there was no apparent reason Schulte was placed under arrest and taken to the sheriff's department. He was not told why he was under arrest. Schulte remained locked up in the Hondo jail for two days. Then he was then taken to the San Antonio State Mental Hospital. He was placed on an involuntary psychiatric hold. In 1974, it was easy for a sheriff to pick up anyone he deemed "crazy." Without any evidence or cause, a person could be committed to the state hospital until he or she proved they were not crazy. Schulte said after several months he was released from the hospital. The doctors told him he was "now cured." Schulte said being locked up in a mental hospital taught him a lesson. He decided to keep his mouth shut as long as Charlie Hitzfelder Sr. was the sheriff of Medina County.

In 1981, twenty years later and following the election of a new sheriff, Schulte came forward. He reached out to a reserve deputy and local pharmacist he knew. He confided to Bill Butler the secret he kept all those years. In short order, Butler called Sheriff Campsey and told him Schulte had a story to tell. After many interviews of Schulte over the years, Sheriff Campsey believed most of John's story. To this day Campsey believes some of events happened as Schulte reported. The only problem for the new sheriff was what kind of witness would Schulte be with a record of incarceration for mental problems?

In 1962, Pauline Sanchez, a classmate of Carolyn, came forward. She told Hondo Police that on the night of Carolyn's disappearance, she had spoken with Carolyn. Carolyn told Pauline that she was going to see her boyfriend and they planned to run away to Louisiana. The Hondo Police chief passed this information to Sheriff Charlie. There is no record that Sheriff Charlie ever interviewed Pauline Sanchez.

FIVE
Locked-up in Midland
Dennis Heyen Remembers His Living Hell

In 2009, Dennis Heyen spoke about his arrest in November 1961 for the murder of Carolyn Covey. At the time of Carolyn's disappearance, Dennis worked at Howard's Gulf Station in Hondo, pumping gas and performing minor mechanical work for Howard's station. He also washed cars when needed. Dennis knew Claudette Carolyn Covey. He helped her with her homework on several occasions. Dennis and Carolyn were friends and also dated on occasion. At the same time Dennis dated Carolyn, she went out with other local boys. Dennis said that Junior Hitzfelder and Rodney Freeman were two local boys who dated Carolyn.

He remembers to this day what Carolyn told him. She said that on several occasions Sheriff Charlie approached Carolyn and ordered Carolyn to stay away from his son. Carolyn said that the sheriff told her that she was "no good" and did not want his son around her.

On the night Carolyn disappeared, Dennis specifically remembered that she was still involved with Junior. According to Dennis, Junior, like his father, felt that he was better than Carolyn. However, Junior kept seeing her—even though he thought he was superior to her. The financial status of people often came into play in Hondo. Junior's family was well off financially and Carolyn's family was poor. Even the high school aged kids, often said bad things to poorer kids in town. Carolyn told Dennis that she was afraid of sheriff Charlie. Dennis said that "everyone" in town was aware Sheriff Charlie was a crooked sheriff and a man that shouldn't be crossed.

Dennis related that the last time he saw Carolyn was on Valentine's Day, the very night she disappeared. Carolyn was walking near the Gulf station—headed towards US 90. Dennis was working his job at the Gulf station that night. He saw Carolyn, and yelled out to her as she walked by. She yelled out to him that she was going to Lenny Wannet's place, a small Drive Inn beer joint and market. Lenny's sold sundries and was the only place open at night. Dennis never saw Carolyn alive after this encounter. He also remembered seeing Carolyn with Junior the night before on February 13, 1961. Dennis was positive then, and to this day, is "100%" positive that Junior was in town, with Carolyn that night.

Dennis got off work at 9 PM almost every night. He also recalled that on Valentine's night Carolyn's sisters came by the station looking for her. Barbara Covey wanted to know if Dennis had seen her. Dennis told Barbara that he had seen Carolyn walking towards Highway 90, a few hours earlier--but didn't see her return towards her house. Dennis mentioned to Barbara that Junior and Carolyn were at the station the night before. Junior had pulled into the station, and Carolyn jumped into the car with him. He suggested that maybe she was out riding around with Junior. Barbara confided that they were worried about Carolyn and asked him to call their house if he saw her.

Later that night, as Dennis was closing up the station, Albert Covey, Carolyn's father also came by the station looking for Carolyn. Dennis said that by then, he was worried about her and offered to help. He later rode around all night with Dewey and Alice, looking for Carolyn. Dennis and Albert spent the entire night scouring the town in a vain attempt to find Carolyn.

Dennis described Junior Hitzfelder as a "loner" and someone not well liked around town. He personally believed that Junior was a homosexual or bisexual.

Dennis said that the boys in school around Charlie's age were always afraid of sheriff Charlie. Because of their fears, some felt that if they got along with Junior, they would get along with Charlie. The sheriff liked to stop boys driving around town for any little infraction. The boys thought that by being friendly with Junior they could possibly ward off any unwanted attention from the sheriff.

Because Junior was a "bad person" in Dennis' mind, he often told Carolyn to stay away from him. Carolyn was a sweet girl according to Dennis, but at the same time, she was a "free spirit" and different from other Hondo girls. Her friendliness left her open to be taken advantage of by some of the boys. Dennis said that Carolyn often came to Dennis' house, and he would help her with homework. He confided that although he was 5 years older than Carolyn, they went out together on occasion. He admitted that they did have sex on occasion

After Carolyn disappeared, Sheriff Charlie frequently came to the Gulf station and peppered Dennis with questions. Dennis believed that sheriff Charlie was trying to "pin" Carolyn's disappearance on him. Over and over again, sheriff Charlie would show up at his work and would ask Dennis, "Where did you put her body?" Even before Carolyn's body was found in Yancey, sheriff Charlie kept trying to get him to confess to taking her. Almost daily Charlie would try to scare Dennis.

It became apparent that the sheriff would never leave him alone. Charlie would even follow Dennis around town. Then one day, the sheriff told Dennis, "I'm going to tell you a story. I've seen a lot of executions in my life, and I know you haven't seen any. Did you know your eyes pop out when they electrocute you?" Dennis told Sheriff Charlie he was not going to be scared by him.

Finally, the harassment had become unbearable, forcing Dennis to leave his job at the Gulf station. Jack Howard, the station's owner told Dennis, he was tired of all the unwarranted attention by the sheriff. He said that the sheriff coming into the station daily was bad for his business. Dennis, fearing being fired got another job, but Charlie began coming around that job almost daily as well. Finally, Dennis got a third station job and worked there for a few months. Charlie continued to really pour on the harassment, threatening Dennis constantly. The sheriff told him he was going take him into the country and beat the hell out of him, or hang Dennis over a tree and shoot him. Back then, Dennis said he wasn't afraid of anyone but his father. The sheriff harassed Dennis so much, he couldn't work. He repeatedly told Charlie that he didn't know anything about Carolyn's disappearance.

Finally, the sheriff was able to get to Dennis. After work, Dennis went home and told his father that Sheriff Charlie was bothering him every day. He told his dad that he could not stand the pressure any longer. Charlie was making his life a living hell. Dennis told his father that the sheriff treated him so badly he could no longer stand it. Dennis told his dad he made up his mind and was leaving town. His father warned him that leaving would make it look as if he had something to do with Carolyn's disappearance.

Dennis left Hondo and went to Denver City, Texas, located on west of Midland, Texas near the Snyder, oil field. When Dennis left town, Carolyn had not yet been found.

One fall day in 1961, after Halloween, Dennis was working in the Snyder Oil fields working on an oil rig. On this day, Dennis was one hundred feet in the air on an oil rig. Dennis saw red lights, like those on police cars coming toward the rig. The cars drove up to the oil rig Dennis was working on. When the police got out of their cars, they pointed rifles and guns at Dennis, ordering him off the rig. When Dennis came down he was arrested for the murder of Carolyn Covey. By now, Dennis had heard that they had found Carolyn's remains. He asked the police how Carolyn was killed and why he was being arrested. They would not say how she was murdered. They asked Dennis if he owned a knife. It was common for a rig driller to have a knife, and Dennis gave his up. The police then asked Dennis if he owed a gun. He told the police over and over that he did not own a gun.

The police handcuffed Dennis and took him to the Department of Public Safety in Midland, Texas. Dennis was first put into a cell alone. Soon afterwards, Dennis was moved to a larger cell with several other prisoners. The jailer told the other prisoners that Dennis was "convicted of murdering a little girl". The inmates gave Dennis a terrifying look. Dennis was smart enough to know what happens in jail when you are charged as a child-killer.

Sheriff Charlie showed up at the jail an hour or so after Dennis arrived at the jail. Dennis related that the next two days were a living hell for him.

Sheriff Charlie and a Texas Ranger "questioned" Dennis

continuously for two straight days. At one point during the questioning, Dennis told Charlie that on the night before Carolyn disappeared, his son, Junior, had picked Carolyn up. Charlie screamed at Dennis, calling him a liar. He denied that his son was in town. Charlie yelled to Dennis, "My son was in California in the Navy that night". Again, Dennis told the sheriff in no uncertain terms that Junior was at his station when Carolyn disappeared. Charlie went ballistic. Dennis was afraid that Charlie would shoot him as he sat in the jail. As the interrogation went on, Dennis told Charlie that he helped look for Carolyn the night she disappeared.

He told Charlie that when Carolyn didn't come home as expected, he knew deep inside that something was wrong. Carolyn would have only have gotten in the car with somebody, if she knew them. He was worried something had happened to her. He told Charlie that they looked around town for Carolyn all night. He hoped that someone would find her. When they checked back at the Covey house, there was no news. They continued looking. They looked for Carolyn all night until sunrise.

The second morning Dennis was in jail, he was given a polygraph. The examiner kept the results from him. After the polygraph test, Sheriff Charlie came in to the room. He told Dennis to confess to what he had done to Carolyn. Dennis responded by telling the examiner that he would never hurt Carolyn and that he was innocent.

He reminded Sheriff Charlie that Carolyn was his friend his, and a friend of his family. This did not mean anything to Charlie who continued to question Dennis over a period of several hours. Finally, Sheriff Charlie put a cigarette in Dennis' mouth and lit it. Dennis was still handcuffed to a chair and couldn't use his hand. He was sitting in the chair and smoking the cigarette when a Texas Ranger came in the room. The ranger asked Dennis who gave him the cigarette. Before Dennis or anyone could say a word, the Ranger suddenly and violently hit Dennis upside his head. The cigarette flew out of his mouth.

Charlie and the ranger repeated this cruel exercise throughout the day. Charlie would give Dennis one cigarette after another. Charlie would leave the room and the ranger would step in and smack Dennis. Finally, Dennis told Charlie not to put a cigarette in his mouth again.

Dennis said that Sheriff Charlie and the ranger would play good cop/bad cop. Finally, out of shear frustration, Dennis told the sheriff, “Let me tell you exactly how it is. I no longer care if you beat me. I didn’t kill Carolyn.” They were not going to make him say he did.

Dennis told Charlie, “The night that Carolyn went missing she walked behind my station, and your son was in town that night.” Dennis declared that Junior was in town the night before as well, and he saw her jump in Charlie’s car at the station. Charlie became furious again. He yelled at Dennis and threatened to “hurt him”.

Dennis was interrogated for two days. Face slapping was not the only physical abuse he endured. Dennis said that the lawmen constantly slapped him around. He recalled that his mistreatment went on hour after hour. He summarized the treatment by saying “the lawmen beat the hell out of him”. It did not matter which officer was in the room. Each would beat him, except Charlie, who acted like he cared for Dennis. Dennis saw through the sheriff’s deception.

He told Sheriff Charlie they could continue beating him, but he was innocent. He told them they were not going to make him say he killed Carolyn. Finally out of pure frustration, Dennis told the sheriff he knew he was a crooked sheriff. He told Charlie that when Charlie came into the stations where Dennis worked, he learned quickly that he was taking money. He laid out the sheriff’s scam. Charlie would tell the station owners he wanted to buy a set of tires for his Medina County car. Charlie would fill out a request for payment from the county, but never take delivery of the tires. Charlie would pocket the money from the stations and have the owners bill the county to get their money back. The station owners gave the sheriff the money, no questions asked. Dennis said he kept records of every transaction Sheriff Charlie made. Charlie also got free gasoline from the stations. When Charlie came into a station for gasoline, the owner would fill out a receipt. Knowing he would never get paid, the owner threw out the receipt. Dennis would collect the receipt and put it in his pocket.

Dennis told the sheriff he had a stack of receipts three or four inches high. He warned Charlie that he knew what kind of a crook he was, keeping every receipt the sheriff generated.

Telling Charlie this made him go crazy. Dennis told Charlie he was going to turn the receipts over to Hondo authorities. The sheriff was furious. Dennis intended to make Charlie angry. In the 1960s, people generally respected the police, but Dennis knew how powerful and corrupt the sheriff was. However, Dennis was more afraid of his father than he was of any law enforcement officer in the country. Charlie got more out of the community than free gas. Almost everything was free for his wife and children at the stores in town. The sheriff would walk in and take whatever he wanted. Business owners were afraid to charge the sheriff or challenge him.

For two days Dennis was not allowed to sleep. Just when he thought the rough treatment was over, they would begin again. During the ordeal, Dennis wore dirty clothes from the oil field, not being allowed to change into dry clean clothes. He does not remember eating anything. Dennis believes his release came after a newspaper reporter arrived from Odessa or Midland. The reporter was asking about the boy from Hondo who was arrested for the Covey murder. Sheriff Charlie and the reporter were standing outside the door where Dennis was being questioned. Dennis did not know if it was for his benefit, but he heard Charlie tell the reporter that Dennis didn't do it, and that there was no way he could have done it. The newsman left and Dennis thought to himself, "Oh thank god, thank god." He was so relieved.

Dennis recalled that the lawmen came back into the room and grabbed him again. They took him aside for one more beating and then told him he was free to go. Dennis asked how he was going to get back to the oil fields. The DPS officers were just going to turn him loose on the street. Dennis was afraid that somebody might drive by and shoot him. Dennis asked again how he was going to get back to his job. He was told he had to make it back on his own. It was a long way back to the oil rig, 170 miles or more. Finally, a DPS trooper agreed to take Dennis back to the oil rig. When Dennis arrived at the oil field, the workers were just getting ready to leave for the day. The workers asked Dennis what had happened.

He told them a girl got killed when he was in Hondo and that he was being blamed for the murder.

The workers didn't say much to Dennis. One drove him back to his apartment. When they arrived at Dennis's apartment, the worker told Dennis to look over, just outside his apartment. Someone had taken all his clothes, dumping them in the parking lot. His personal belongings were thrown everywhere. Whoever did this destroyed everything Dennis owned. The receipts he had collected involving the sheriff were now missing. Dennis was 100% positive that Sheriff Charlie personally ransacked his apartment to find the incriminating receipts. While picking up his belongings, the lady who managed his apartment told Dennis to get his stuff, leave, and never come back. He tried to tell her what happened, but she would not listen.

Dennis drove to the driller's office to get his paycheck. The boss told him he was fired and to get out of town. Dennis was handed his paycheck and told never to return. Dennis was run out of town. He got in his car and took what money he had, and drove back to Hondo. When Dennis got home, he went around back to the bunk house where he and his brothers slept.

Dennis saw his father coming out to the bunk house with a baseball bat in his hands. When he reached Dennis, he told him to leave and never come back. Dennis pleaded with his father and asked what he was going to do. Dennis' brothers warned him that their father was liable to hit him. Dennis knew his father and decided it was best for him to move on. It was apparent to Dennis that Sheriff Charlie told his father he had been arrested.

Dennis had his own theories on who may have killed Carolyn. Charlie Lutz, in his mind, was a good suspect. Dennis used to work at Lutz's Service Station. He worked for him for a few years and said that Charlie Lutz was a perverted piece of crap. Lutz had a glass door in his restroom. He had opaque glass on the walls. The high school cheerleaders would use the restroom to change from their street clothes into their cheerleader outfits. According to Dennis, Lutz would stand outside that door masturbating while the girls changed. Dennis said that Lutz repeated this behavior with just about any female, even fifty- and sixty-year-old women. If

Dennis brought a girlfriend into the station, Lutz would jump into the back seat and paw her. Dennis thought that Charlie Lutz could be a suspect because he was a pervert. Dennis said Lutz rode around town all night, trying to pick up girls, Mexican girls usually. He thought Lutz might have picked up Carolyn, raped her, got scared and killed her. Dennis said that Sheriff Charlie Hitzfelder and Charlie Lutz were very good friends. He did not know if they ever investigated Charlie Lutz.

Dennis also believed Charlie Hitzfelder Jr. could have been involved in the murder of Carolyn Covey. Charlie knew well the county road where Carolyn was found. This was where Charlie Jr. and Pete Hartman used to go to drink beer. He added that they were both town drunks. Dennis said Charlie was seeing Carolyn and was in town when she disappeared

Dennis thought of Carolyn and her murder almost daily. His father disowned him, he lost his jobs, and people thought he did something wrong. All of this was because Sheriff Charlie was a crook. Sheriff Charlie has made Dennis' life a living hell, and still today, 40 plus years later, he is still affected by Sheriff Charlie. Dennis said that his father died several years after he was told to leave home. He was never able to reconcile with his father.

The Sheriff Throws a Shutout!

For the next two years, Sheriff Hitzfelder continued to make a public show of his interest in solving the Covey murder. If someone was arrested in the southwest portion of the United States for kidnapping and/or murdering a young girl, he would be sure to question this man about the Covey murder. This went on for the next few years, until Carolyn's murder seemed to be forgotten by the press in San Antonio and in Hondo. As the years passed, many moved on with their lives, but Carolyn's family never forgot. Her murder had become notorious in the county. Several honest lawmen in and around Hondo did their very best to track suspects. One of these men was Hondo Police Chief Jerome "Jerry" Blinka.

Chief Blinka was the only policeman in Hondo in 1961, but he did employ a night watchman who drove around town making sure business doors were locked. On the evening that Carolyn went missing, Chief Blinka happened to be at the County Sheriff's office. Blinka said that Sheriff Hitzfelder and Deputy O.W. Swatzell were nowhere to be found.

On the night Carolyn went missing, Albert Covey drove to the sheriff's office to report her disappearance. Chief Blinka personally searched the town over and over that night. No one from the Sheriff's Department was interested in Carolyn Covey's disappearance. Chief Blinka said that in June of 1962, he thought he had developed a possible suspect, a man named William Kneeling. Kneeling lived in the Dallas/Fort Worth area. Chief Blinka said he received a tip from Ed Haynes, who had information on Kneeling. He passed the information about Kneeling to Deputy Swatzell. Swatzell was supposed to investigate, but when Blinka asked the sheriff about Kneeling, the sheriff knew nothing about the man or the information that was provided to his deputy.

Later, he asked Swatzell how the information checked out. O.W. told him that Kneeling checked out okay. When he heard about this, he wondered about the sheriff's real interest in the Covey case. The sheriff and his deputy seemed disinterested from the beginning in the Covey murder. Covey family members told him many times that the sheriff was cold to them and did not seem to care about Carolyn's disappearance and later her murder. During the nine months Carolyn was missing, Chief Blinka forwarded information to the sheriff until the day Carolyn's remains were found. The sheriff was evasive and would change the subject. Blinka felt the sheriff should be part of the search, since it was within his jurisdiction. However, the sheriff took control of the case and did all he could to keep the chief out of the loop. After Carolyn's body was found the Sheriff's Department did not inform Chief Blinka. It was not until the next day that the chief heard from townsfolk that Carolyn's body had been located. When he learned the sheriff left him out of the discovery, he confronted the sheriff. He asked him how long he was going to keep him in the dark. The sheriff apologized, saying that he had just been busy. The next morning, Blinka was permitted to go to the crime scene with the DPS crime lab, the Texas Rangers, and the sheriff. For about a week, Blinka was permitted to work on the case. During that week, he learned more about the case from people in town, than he did from the sheriff.

Blinka even heard that the sheriff and/or his family might be involved in the murder. It was clear that Blinka was being kept out of the case. Over the next month, he summarized all the information that he had heard and developed. He came to the conclusion that the sheriff was intentionally ignoring information developed in Hondo. He was more interested in information far away from town. He also noticed that Deputy Swatzell showed little interested in the Covey case. In December 1961, Texas Rangers asked Blinka to check out all the motel registries in Hondo. All of the other motels complied, except for a small motel that O.W. Swatzell owned. Blinka thought this was strange. He asked Swatzell several times to bring him his motel register, but he never complied.

O.W.'s wife alleged that her husband had committed Carolyn's murder, and that he was having relations with his daughter-in-law. He asked the sheriff about this, and the sheriff admitted that some of the rumors about his deputy were true. The sheriff said he told O.W. to quit or he would be fired. He later heard that the sheriff was making accusations against Ed Haynes. Ed had only provided information on the case. The sheriff was spreading rumors that Ed was a window peeper, a burglary suspect, and he did not pay his debts. These were all lies. He knew, because he checked Ed Haynes out himself.

The sheriff was trying to shut Ed out. The sheriff either resented Ed's information or was upset that someone else in town was working on the case. It was clear that the sheriff could not be trusted, so Blinka withheld most of the information he developed about William Kneeling. Later, the sheriff decided to go to Dallas and give Kneeling a polygraph test. Blinka told the sheriff that he wanted to attend the polygraph. Blinka learned later that the sheriff went to Dallas without him to conduct the test along with the DPS.

Blinka said he had questions for Kneeling. It was apparent that he was once again being left out of the loop. He was wondered why the sheriff was shutting him out of the case.

Unexpectedly, Blinka was called into a private city council meeting in June 1962. When he got to the meeting, he was told the council had received creditable information that Blinka was a corrupt chief of police. He was told he would be suspended without pay until further notice. He asked who provided the information to the council. He was told that the sheriff had made certain allegations. They would not go into the allegations at that time. It was clear that the sheriff had him suspended because he was getting too close to the truth. Jerry Blinka was so concerned that there was some kind of cover-up going on that he wrote a letter to the Department of Public Safety Director Col. Homer Garrison. He wanted the director to be notified of his findings so that someone from outside the Medina County Sheriff's Department could properly investigate Carolyn's murder. Jerry Blinka was never reinstated as chief of police of Hondo. Jerry Blinka died of natural causes in the middle 1980s, never knowing for sure who killed Carolyn Covey.

In 1977, Sheriff Butch Campsey reopened the unsolved Carolyn Covey murder case for further investigation. He learned that one of Sheriff Hitzfelder's former deputies might have some information regarding the Covey murder. Bill Scheel was chief deputy for Sheriff Hitzfelder for about five years. He worked for Charlie from 1969-74.When Sheriff Hitzfelder's Chief Deputy Floyd Williamson passed away; the sheriff promoted Bill Scheel to chief deputy. Butch learned that Bill Scheel was still working and living in San Antonio. Butch called Bill on the phone and made arrangements to meet him in San Antonio. Although Bill Scheel did not work for Medina County in 1961, he was aware of Carolyn Covey's murder. Bill had often discussed the Covey case with his good friend Floyd Williamson. Bill Scheel was at the sheriff's office when Ranger Joaquin Jackson came to visit. Floyd and Joaquin were discussing the Covey case and Floyd told Joaquin he would like to solve the murder. Listening to them talk about the case, Bill became interested in it. After that day, he started doing some investigating. He thought more could be done to find the killer. But only after a few days, Bill was called to the sheriff's office over the radio. When he arrived, Sheriff Charlie ordered Bill to drive up to Medina Lake with him. Bill did not ask why they were going to the lake. He knew better than to question the sheriff about anything he said or did. They drove up to the lake and parked. The sheriff stared out at the water and told Bill, "There are many bodies at the bottom of the lake." He observed that they were close to Mexico and he could hire someone to murder a person for $50. He told Bill that if someone reopens the Covey murder case, people would be hurt. Charlie said all this in a low, even tone. Scheel knew what he meant. It was clear to him that he should keep his nose out of the case. Charlie was that way. He could get his point across, making it sound like he was talking at dinner about the pot roast. Bill got the message.

Charlie started driving again and said his son had been nothing but trouble for many years. The sheriff said that maybe he should just let the law pick him up the next time he got into trouble. Bill told Butch Campsey, after this all occurred, that working as a deputy sheriff in Medina County was not a very good idea. Bill resigned from his job and moved away from the area.

SIX
Skeletal Remains
December 16, 1979

In 1979, the author was working as a detective sergeant for the Brazoria County Sheriff. On December 16 around 2 PM he received a radio call dispatching him to County Road 82 and SH6 in Manvel, Texas. A body had been found.

The crime scene was a small rental farmhouse located on CR82, seventy-five yards north of SH6. Joe Duran and his family lived in the rundown house. Debris and trash was strewn around the front porch where Mr. Duran was drinking a beer upon arrival. Standing next to Joe was his teenage daughter, Linda. She was seventeen, about 5’4” tall and weighed 105 pounds. Linda had dark brown, shoulder length hair, and an olive complexion. It was learned that the family dog had apparently found human bones in the adjacent field. The family had never been in the field next to her house, but they recalled a foul smell coming from it a few months earlier. Linda and her family theorized that something died in the field. She recalled how her family avoided that side of the house due to the bad smell. At the time, the author did not know that Linda would soon play a part in the thirty-year quest by this author to solve Carolyn Covey’s murder, as well as the murders of many young girls in the Houston and Galveston during the period of 1971-85.

Mr. Duran pointed to the left side of the house, toward a fenced-in pasture with recently mowed grass. One of his children was on his knees poking a human skull with a long tree branch while another held back an excited medium-sized dog.

Joe Duran said the property owner had recently cut the weeds in the field next to the Duran home. The Duran dog was apparently out scavenging and retrieved the skull, dropping it in the front yard. The skull appeared to be from a young child. The lower jaw was missing from the skull, but the upper teeth were intact and free of any noticeable dental work. A closer examination revealed two small-caliber bullet holes in the bottom rear of the skull. The cause of death had to be murder. The skull was a little weathered, perhaps by exposure to sunlight. It was estimated that the skull had been lying in the field for a year, maybe two.

Over the next few hours a crime scene search was conducted. A few rib bones and vertebrae were found in the area. A diagram of the location of bones was drawn. Mr. Duran and his family were questioned. No one in the family could offer anything helpful about how the skull ended up in the field. Crime scene photos were taken and the remains were put into plastic and paper bags. While at the Duran house, Detective Skarka asked Detective Harry Stiles for his advice on several issues. Detective Skarka returned to the office to write a report. Detective Skarka was not aware that the bodies of scores of young girls had been found in Brazoria County during the previous eight years. For unknown reason, other detectives did not think it important to tell Skarka about similar murders in Brazoria County. Why other detectives failed to mention those unsolved homicides in Harris, Brazoria, and Galveston counties is still a mystery.

In 1979, law enforcement lacked computers and databases. Information on crime patterns was gleaned from monthly bulletins from the Texas Department of Public Safety. Teletype machines sent information to law enforcement agencies, but teletypes from previous crimes were kept in the dispatcher's office. Dispatch was usually off limits. An investigator working a case developed information on similar, previous crimes without much assistance from fellow investigators. There was not much communication or cooperation between investigators and neighboring law enforcement agencies.

This case was a murder in Detective Skarka's mind, but the discovery was never classified that way. To this day the case remains unsolved and the girl's remains unidentified. There is no way to fully disclose the number of murders in and around Brazoria County. County sheriffs protect this information for political reasons: to keep the crime statistics low. In Brazoria County alone, there were at least ten skeletal-remains cases that never received the attention they deserved. A former official in the department recently confirmed the situation. This official still has friends in the department and did not want to go on the record. Boxes of unidentified bones may yet remain in police evidence rooms throughout the region. Self-imposed roadblocks by law enforcement officers have probably hindered the arrest of many killers.

This observation is not meant to discredit the abilities of investigators. Investigators will agree that if remains are never identified, there is no "named" victim. If there is no victim, there is no crime. And if there is no crime, there is no investigation. In police work, to solve a murder, the victim must be identified. If you cannot identify the victim, it is very difficult to identify a killer.

A few weeks after the girl's body was found near the Duran home, another investigator forwarded an attribute and artifacts chart to the DPS Crime Analysis Unit in Austin. He had requested modus operandi (method of operation) similarities from their researchers. Detective Skarka also sent a request to the DPS asking for similar cases in the area.

Twenty-six years later Detective Skarka finally received a list of homicide victims from Brazoria County killed before 1979: Some of the murdered girls were, Nina Lynn Kluge, Collette Wilson, and Kimberly Pitchford. This information would have been very helpful at the time of the investigation, but it never came into Skarka's hands. That was the way things were done at that time. The cold, hard truth was that if a body was found, and the body could not be identified, not much effort went into identifying a suspect. Without missing person reports, little could be done to identify the body. Law enforcement officials felt that skeletal remains meant the victims were nameless. Therefore, there was no suspect, no evidence, and finally, no proof of a crime at all. The politics of the day required that the sheriff look like he had crime under control. A sheriff's goal was to be reelected every four years. Newspaper and television reports of unsolved murders of young girls would make a sitting sheriff look bad. The unsolved murder of several dead girls was a recipe for losing an election. Investigators were told to keep their cases to themselves. Losing your job was easy back then. You worked at the pleasure of the sheriff. He could work you seventy hours a week without paying you overtime, or fire you on a whim.

The initial report, completed by the author on the body found near the Duran home, listed the remains as homicide. Working on this case file, Detective Skarka was awakened to the unbelievable reality of selective classification of a crime. His supervisor demanded he classify the case as skeletal remains. The supervisor asked how Skarka knew this was a murder case. Two bullet holes in the back of the skull certainly pointed to murder. The supervisor's response was swift, "Tell me how you know that this was a murder?" The supervisor speculated that the bones could have come from an old grave. The grave could have been dug up by varmints. Or a hunter shooting at skunks or other varmints could have hit the skull. This was more than a subtle hint that little or no time should be spent on this case. Even though warned, Detective Skarka set out to identify the murdered girl. A few weeks later a letter from the Department of Public Safety's Crime Analysis Unit arrived. There was a possible similar crime - an unsolved homicide of a fourteen-year-old girl in Hondo, Texas.

Claudette Carolyn Covey was reported missing on Valentines Day 1961. Her skeletal remains were found in a field, just off a county road in rural Yancey in Medina County. Like the Duran remains, Carolyn's body was found with two small-caliber bullet holes in the back of her skull. The Texas Rangers, at one point, suspected a young man named Charles Hitzfelder Jr. The DPS recommended contacting Texas Ranger H. Joaquin Jackson at the Uvalde Ranger Station. The letter said he would have more detailed information of possible similarities. Ranger Jackson was contacted that same day. He was told about the Brazoria County case. Jackson listened intently, not asking any questions until he heard all the case information.

He told the author that Charlie Hitzfelder's father was the sheriff of Medina County until 1977.

At one point, the Texas Rangers thought Charlie Jr. had something to do with her murder, but because his father was sheriff, there was not much they could do. Ranger Jackson reported that a new sheriff, Butch Campsey, had been elected in 1977. The Medina County Sheriff's Department was called and a message was left for Sheriff Butch Campsey. A few hours later, Detective Skarka and Butch Campsey spoke for the first time and the two immediately connected. It was clear that Butch suspected Charlie Jr. and/or his family may have been involved in the disappearance and murder of Carolyn Covey. Butch had recently learned that Charlie Jr. lived in Galveston County just off Highway 6. Highway 6 runs from Manvel to Galveston County. Junior lived only twenty miles south of the Manvel crime scene. This was a very odd coincidence. Butch agreed to meet at the Brazoria County Sheriff's office.

It was early February 1980. Butch Campsey and a fellow lawman, Frank Perkins, arrived at the Sheriff's Department. Butch Campsey did not look like the stereotypical Texas sheriff. Butch stood about 5'8" tall, although he insists 5'8½" tall. He weighed about 165 pounds. Butch wore a nice Stetson and cowboy boots. He had a sheriff's badge pinned to his shirt. There was no gun on his hip. Skarka thought Campsey must think of himself as Sheriff Andy Taylor from Mayberry. Later, Skarka learned that Butch—for emergencies only, carried a 25-caliber pistol in his boot. It's safe to say that Donald "Butch" Campsey's personality was the main reason he was elected sheriff. He was friendly and very personable. In 1975, Butch was talked into running for sheriff to replace the infamous, some say corrupt, Sheriff Charles Hitzfelder Sr. There was a long history of the corruption during the Hitzfelder years. Many in Medina County believe Junior or someone in his family killed Carolyn Covey. Butch was a young boy when Carolyn went missing, but remembered her disappearance and the discovery of Carolyn's body.

After discussing the Covey case and the new case, the three police officers drove to Manvel, where the skeleton remains were found near the Duran family home. The family was re-interviewed. A later visit to Galveston County was discussed to check out where Charlie Jr. was living. At the Duran home, Linda Duran and her mother Sally were re-interviewed. Sally said she had no idea how the bones ended up in front of her house. Linda Duran commented about a strange man that she met who took her out on dates.

When asked why this man was strange, she volunteered that he kept a gun in his car, and that he was always trying to have sex with her. This man was much older than she was and she felt he was a little weird. She met the man hitchhiking from Alvin one day. He picked her up and brought her home that afternoon. Linda said the man's name was Chuck or Charlie. She said he lived on Highway 6 near Galveston.

When Linda said the name Charlie, bells went off in the investigators' heads. Linda described him as about thirty-five years old with brown haircut in a mullet, and a mustache. He told Linda that he drove trucks and liked to pick up hitchhikers. The man's face was pocked-marked with creepy-looking eyes. She thought he was weird, but nice to her, so she went out with him. Charlie would give her beer to drink and on occasion they smoked pot. The first time he picked up Linda hitchhiking, he was nice to her. When they got to her house, Linda's mother came outside and met Charlie. Sally also thought Charlie was a nice man. He asked Linda out for dinner that night. Sally said it would be okay. Later that night, Charlie came back to the house. He was still driving his white pickup truck, but had changed his clothes. He took Linda into Houston to the El Chico's Mexican Restaurant for dinner.

After dinner, Charlie stopped at a store and bought some beer. He asked Linda how old she was. When Linda first met Charlie she was only fifteen. She lied and told Charlie she was almost eighteen. The two drove around and he offered her some beer. After awhile, they parked on a county road and smoked some marijuana. While they were sitting and talking, Charlie asked her if she would give him oral sex. Linda refused, explaining that she did not know him well enough. She remembered his words, "I just want you to give me a blow job." She told Charlie she did not do that type of thing, and he got angry with her. About that time, a car drove by slowly and the driver looked at them both. Seeing this, Charlie started up his truck and drove Linda home. He dropped her off and left. Linda was afraid, but did not say anything to her mother about what Charlie had asked her to do. This was not the last time Linda saw Charlie. There were a few more encounters over a period of months.

About two weeks after their first date, Linda was sitting on her front porch around 3:30 PM. Charlie drove up with another young girl in his truck. Her name was "Tricia" and her brown hair framed a very pretty face. She was seventeen and from somewhere near Texas City. Charlie invited Linda to go to Houston with them. They were going to the Time Tunnel to listen to music and play games. Linda felt safe and agreed to go. They stayed at the Time Tunnel for a few hours playing the amusement games. Charlie had some marijuana with him and said they could smoke it on the way home. The trio left and headed back to Manvel. When they got to Pearland, Charlie stopped at a store to get some beer. He and Tricia went into the store, while Linda waited in the truck. Linda had to tie her shoelace. As she bent down, she saw a gun under Charlie's seat. She was curious and touched the gun to see if it was real. The gun was real. As Linda put the gun back under the seat, Tricia and Charlie came out of the store. They were bickering over something. He was trying to kiss Tricia, but she kept pulling away from him. When they got into the truck, Tricia was mad about something, but did not say anything. Instead of stopping to drink beer or smoke marijuana, Charlie drove Linda home. No one said anything during the ride back. Charlie was angry and Tricia was upset. Linda sat silently until Charlie got her home. After dropping Linda off, he peeled out as he drove away.

A few weeks later, Charlie came by the house once again. He parked out front and honked his horn. Linda looked out the door and saw it was Charlie. She came out and asked him what was up. He asked her to go for a ride because he was sad about something. Linda agreed and got into his truck. She saw that Chuck had severe scratch on his right arm. Linda asked about the scratch, and Chuck said "the scratch had nothing to with Tricia". Linda asked Charlie how Tricia was doing. He told Linda he was not seeing Tricia any longer. Charlie told Linda not to worry about Tricia. He said he would not hurt Tricia, and that he was a good boy, adding that his father was the sheriff in San Antonio. He told Linda that he and Tricia did not get along. This admission alarmed Linda, but she thought he must be okay because he was a sheriff's son. She got in his truck and they drove into Alvin. Charlie bought a 12-pack of beer and seemed upset as they just drove some county roads. Linda was concerned about this.

After awhile, he asked Linda if she wanted to drive to Galveston to visit the beach. Linda told Charlie she would have to ask her mother. He seemed surprised to learn her mother was home. He told Linda he had better take her home. On the way home, Charlie admitted to Linda that he did not get along with his father and that his mother also got mad at him when he was a boy. He said he was thinking about moving back to San Antonio to drive trucks. When they got to her house, Charlie tried to kiss Linda, but she refused. Charlie became angry, and Linda quickly got out of the truck. He peeled out as he left. That was the last time she saw Charlie. She never saw Tricia again either.

To investigators, it was clear Linda was being truthful. Her description of the man called Charlie pointed to Hitzfelder. Linda knew too much personal information for her story to be untrue. A few days later, Linda was asked to look at photographs to see if she could identify Charlie. A photo spread, including a recent photo of Charlie Hitzfelder Jr., was put together. The three men in the photo line up were all similar looking. She was asked if the man she knew as Charlie was in any of the photos. Linda immediately pointed at Charlie Hitzfelder's photo. She was positive. As she was pointing at the photo, Linda volunteered that her mother would also be able to pick Charlie out of the line up. Linda's mother took the file folder, examined the photos for about ten seconds and picked the photo of Charlie Hitzfelder Jr.

SEVEN
California Here They Come

On February 18, 1961, Iona and Mary Ruth arrived in San Diego, California. Today, the exact date of their arrival is in dispute. According to Mary Ruth, she and Iona drove from Hondo, Texas, to San Diego in three days. Throughout the journey, Iona never mentioned anything about a missing girl in Hondo. She alluded to something big that had happened in town after calling the sheriff along the way. Mary Ruth was six months pregnant when she left Hondo with Iona. Along the way, Iona confined most of her conversation with Mary Ruth to small talk about the baby. Iona often told Mary Ruth how she was going to be a happy grandmother. She even told Mary Ruth how nice it will be to hold the baby, and how happy she was that she would not have to stay up all night when the baby cried. Mary Ruth was mostly quiet throughout the trip, but always respectful of Iona. She was careful to respond when asked a question. At rest stops and at the motels, Mary Ruth kept to herself. Deep inside, she was concerned about what may occur at the end of her journey. She thought she was in love with Junior but was afraid to be away from her family in Devine. Because Mary Ruth was pregnant, Iona and Mary Ruth took their time driving to California.

The travel distance from Hondo to San Diego is less than 1,300 miles. The trip could have been completed in about twenty-four hours by driving straight through. Mary Ruth said the trip took three days, stopping the first night in El Paso and the second night in Tucson.

Neither Iona nor Mary Ruth was ever questioned officially about the trip. Iona went to her grave without making a statement detailing the trip. Mary Ruth said Junior had just finished several days of boat dock duty when they arrived in San Diego. If this were true, Junior would have had an alibi for February 14, 1961. That Charlie Jr. was in California on that day was an accepted version of events. Today, Mary Ruth insists that when they arrived in San Diego, they met Junior at the Navy base. Charlie told them that he had just completed three days of duty. He could not have possibly been in Hondo. However in 1961, a person could take a commercial jet from San Diego to San Antonio in just hours. Mary Ruth reluctantly agreed to this possibility.

It would have been easy for investigators to backtrack the women's trip. No one ever checked to see if Junior was on the trip with Iona and Mary Ruth. When Butch Campsey took office in 1977, he learned that investigators never checked to see if Iona and Mary Ruth were in town the night Carolyn went missing. Because forty-eight years have passed, no one will ever know for sure. It is clear today that Mary Ruth still stands by her account. She said she would not put anything past Charlie Jr., but she doesn't know how he could have killed Carolyn Covey. There is only one problem with Iona and Mary Ruth's account of Charlie Junior's whereabouts on February 14, 1961.The account is based solely on his statement to his mother and Mary Ruth.

Eighteen years after Carolyn's death, Sheriff Campsey tried to verify Charlie Junior's alibi. Charlie Junior's files were requested from the Navy. Butch was the first to look at the records. Unfortunately, the official files did not record Junior's leave time, his shift changes, or any special arrangements he may have made. The Navy files were considered a dead-end in determining Junior's whereabouts on February 14, 1961.

In writing this book, a former shipmate of Junior's was located. He said the two men served in San Diego at the same time. This sailor said that an enlisted man could easily make changes in his duty dates and times. This practice was common for sailors stationed on shore. It was entirely possible that he could have made arrangements to have someone trade one of his three-day on and three-day off shifts. This kind of arrangement would give Junior nine days off in a row. If investigators knew this in 1961, they could have easily checked to see if Charlie Jr. took a flight to San Diego in February 1961.

Charlie Jr. could have flown to San Antonio and returned to San Diego in his car with his mother and Mary Ruth. Many people in Hondo believe today that scenario is the truth, finding it hard to believe Charlie would let his mother drive his pregnant wife from Hondo to San Diego. Also, Charlie's car was his pride and joy. The 1956 Chevrolet was Charlie's most important possession. Mary Ruth confirmed this. Charlie Junior's car was his life. Iona and Mary Ruth's trip to California on February 15, 1961 was the start of almost fifty years of speculation and conjecture.

A New Home in California

The first day in California, Iona and Mary Ruth drove to the Navy base and met up with Junior. Junior seemed happy to see his mother, but was somewhat distant toward Mary Ruth. He seemed more interested in the condition of his car. Junior told Iona he found a small apartment near the Navy base. He asked the manager to hold the apartment until his mother came to town, because he did not have money for rent and a deposit. Junior, Iona, and Mary Ruth drove the short distance from the Navy base to the small one-bedroom apartment. It had a view of the San Diego Harbor. Mary Ruth recalled years later that she loved the view. Iona, Mary Ruth, and Junior contacted the manager and asked for the keys to the unit. The manager escorted them to the small, furnished apartment. Iona decided that the apartment suited Junior and Mary Ruth just fine.

They decided to take the apartment. Iona opened her purse and asked the manager how much it would be for two months rent and the deposit. He quoted $150, and Iona peeled out the cash. The young couple had their first home. Iona stayed in California for another day, helping Mary Ruth set up the apartment. On her third day in California, Charlie Jr. and Mary Ruth took Iona to the bus station. Junior thanked his mother again for helping them get started. He told her that he would find some way to repay her. Iona knew better. She just asked that they name their baby after her. Mary Ruth was also grateful for the financial help and told her that she liked the name Iona.

Married Life: It Wasn't Like "Ozzie and Harriet" Charlie Junior's First Marriage

After Iona's departure, Mary Ruth tried her best to settle into her new life. She was happy that she was out of Medina County, but was secretly fearful every day. She wondered how her new life would be. Mary Ruth was young and foolish back then, believing she was in love with Charlie Jr. He had a good side. He was good-looking, not drop-dead good-looking, but he was good-looking. They had fun when they were together in Medina County. The two talked about getting married some day and what they would name their children.

Mary Ruth believes that Junior had some sort of affection for her. Why else would he have this relationship with her? Mary Ruth knew Junior was forced into the marriage because of family honor, not love and commitment. Mary Ruth's daddy threatened to have Junior arrested for statutory rape if he did not wed Mary Ruth. While in California, Mary Ruth spent most of her days alone. She busied herself keeping the apartment clean and making sure dinner was ready on time when Charlie Junior was home. Charlie Junior was still assigned to boats and docks duty, working three days on and three days off. Mary Ruth had no way to go to the base exchange or to the doctor for check-ups. Junior would take his Chevrolet to work, never allowing Mary Ruth to drive his car. On his days off, Charlie Junior would sit in front of the television, smoke cigarettes, and drink beer.

Charlie Junior mostly ignored Mary Ruth. He could be cruel, twisting her arm behind her back while asking if it hurt. Then he would callously tell her it didn't hurt him.

In the evening, Charlie Junior headed downtown, hanging out with sailors in beer joints, pool halls, and movie theaters. On occasion, he would take Mary Ruth. About three weeks after arriving in California, Junior took Mary Ruth on one of his trips to town. Charlie Junior wanted to buy a new pair of jeans, but did not have enough money to pay for the jeans. Junior knew that Mary Ruth's mother gave her some emergency food money. Charlie Junior demanded the money. Mary Ruth's mother warned her to hold onto the money so she would always have food money for herself and the baby. She was afraid to say no to Junior and gave him the money so he could buy the jeans. A day or so later, she admitted to her father on the phone that Charlie Junior used the food money to purchase jeans. Her father was angry. Mary Ruth's mother wondered how Junior could use food money for clothes. She asked how the two were getting along. Mary Ruth told her mother that Charlie Junior was mean to her all the time. She said he could be very cruel. Junior made fun of her, always putting her down. Mary Ruth's mother knew she was not happy being with Charlie Junior, remembering how Junior had once slapped Mary Ruth in the face back in Texas. She told Mary Ruth that Charlie Junior was never concerned about her well being.

Since moving to California, the couple was always broke. Junior spent his money on unimportant things, and soon the couple did not have enough money for food. Her parents convinced Mary Ruth to come home.

Mary Ruth decided to have her baby in Devine. Her parents wired Mary Ruth money for a plane ticket. Once the money arrived, Mary Ruth told Charlie Jr. that she was going back to Texas to finish high school. At first Junior did not want her to leave. Later, Charlie Jr. had a fellow sailor's wife try to talk her into staying. Mary Ruth had already made up her mind to eat right and have a healthy baby. Mary Ruth was seven months pregnant at the end of March 1961 when she returned to Texas. Charlie took her to the airport, and she flew to San Antonio. As he dropped her off, Charlie Junior suggested they get a divorce. At the time, Mary Ruth thought she was still in love with Charlie Jr. so his comment about a divorce hurt her deeply. Mary Ruth was leaving because her parents were afraid she was not eating well. Mary Ruth could not understand why Junior wanted a divorce.

A few months after returning to Texas, Mary Ruth had her baby at Lackland Air Force Hospital. Iona Elizabeth "Beth" Hitzfelder was born on May 17, 1961. Mary Ruth was forced to stay in the hospital for a week after she developed an infection. Charlie Jr. did not call or send a card when the baby was born. After she got out of the hospital, Mary Ruth went home to Devine. The family was a real help with Beth. Mary Ruth wrote letters to Charlie Jr. from the time she went back to Devine until after the baby was born. She does not remember Junior ever replying.

In December 1961, Charlie Junior received leave from the Navy. He returned to Medina County. It was around Christmas. Being young and foolish, Mary Ruth thought she was still in love with Charlie Jr. When he came to Devine, he met his daughter, Beth, for the first time. Mary Ruth and Charlie Jr. got along fairly well while he was on leave. She always felt that Charlie Jr. could be fun at times. However, she recalled that Junior was cheap and spoiled rotten. When Charlie Jr. was growing up, his grandparents spoiled him, giving him anything he wanted. During Charlie Junior's leave, Mary Ruth and Charlie had sex a few times. She became pregnant with Chari, their second daughter. Charlie was not happy about her pregnancy, but there was little Mary Ruth could do. In the 1960s, few women got abortions and Mary Ruth was opposed to abortion. She continued to write to Charlie Junior, keeping him informed about Beth and her pregnancy, but Charlie Jr. never wrote her back.

A few months into her pregnancy, Charlie Jr. called Mary Ruth and said he wanted a divorce. Mary Ruth told Junior she was not opposed to a divorce, but wanted to wait until their baby was born. She wanted her baby to be legitimate. Junior was not happy about her decision, but there was little he could do. In 1962, Mary Ruth returned to school, but struggled to keep up with her studies due to her pregnancy. People in town did not know she was getting a divorce after the baby was born. Everyone thought she was happy in her marriage. In May 1962, Beth had her first birthday. Charlie did not send a card, nor did he call his daughter.

On September 10, 1962, Mary Ruth returned to the Air Force Hospital in San Antonio and gave birth to Chari. Like Beth, Chari was born healthy. After Mary Ruth got out of the hospital, she returned home to Devine to stay with her parents.

Mary Ruth's extended family helped her with the babies, allowing her to finish high school. A few months after Chari was born, Mary Ruth decided to go through with her plans to divorce Charlie. Junior was now stationed aboard the USS Ranger in Alameda, CA, The Ranger was on a tour in the Far East for the next five or six months. Charlie Jr. returned to port in Alameda in June 1963.

Mary Ruth's mother took her to the courthouse in Hondo to file divorce papers. The clerk at the courthouse promised Mary Ruth that when the court date came, she would arrange for Charlie Sr. to be absent. The court clerks and other courthouse workers were afraid of the sheriff. They feared Sheriff Charlie might try to stop the divorce. An effort was made to keep the proceedings from the townspeople.

Charlie Junior was mailed the divorce papers while aboard the USS Ranger. The papers came back without being served. There was a note attached to the papers, indicating Charlie had been arrested and was in the Alameda County Jail. The note did not say what he was arrested for. The papers were resent to the Alameda County jail. The papers came back again. This time, there was a note stating Charlie was now in the Navy brig. After a month or so, Charlie was finally tracked down and served. A few months later, Mary Ruth went to the Hondo Courthouse to have the divorce finalized. Keeping their word, the clerks arranged for Mary Ruth to be in court at about 7 A.M. They told Mary Ruth that the sheriff would not be at the courthouse that early.

The divorce was granted. The judge's order required Charlie to pay $40 a month in child support. Through out Beth and Chari's first 18 years, Mary Ruth never received one cent of child support from Charlie. A few years later, Mary Ruth met a man, fell in love and remarried. The new family moved to San Antonio, about one-half hour drive from Devine. Mary Ruth did not see Charlie again until 1998, a few days before he died.

In 1965, Mary Ruth's new husband wanted to adopt Beth and Chari. Mary Ruth tracked down Charlie Jr. He was now out of the Navy and still living in California. Charlie Jr. had married a woman named Charlene. Mary Ruth's attorney sent Junior papers about the proposed adoption. After Charlie Jr. received the papers, he telephoned Mary Ruth and said he would never allow the adoption. Mary Ruth's mother was furious with Charlie. She called Charlie Junior and reminded him that he had not even met his second daughter. Further, he never paid for any financial support of his children. Charlie still insisted he would not allow the adoption. Mary Ruth decided to have her lawyer take care of the adoption. The lawyer told Mary Ruth that since Charlie had never paid one cent of child support, he owed thousands of dollars in back support. The lawyer wrote Charlie Jr. and informed him that if he did not give up his parental rights, he would be sued for all the child support he had failed to pay. After Charlie got the letter, he immediately called Mary Ruth's attorney and asked if he gave up custody, could he get out of paying the money he owed. The attorney told Charlie Junior that he would no longer be financially responsible for the girls. Charlie Jr. agreed to sign the papers and give up all contact with his children.

Mary Ruth's Life After Charlie

After Mary Ruth's divorce from Charlie Junior, she continued to live in Devine until she remarried in 1965. Although she moved from Devine, she frequently spoke with her old classmates. Mary Ruth's new life took her to several places around the country. After Charlie Junior, Mary Ruth said she was lucky in her choice of men. She did very well financially and politically. She was elected a county commissioner in a large north Texas county. She also served on her county's Republican Committee. Today, Mary Ruth works in the real estate profession and lives near Austin, Texas. Both Beth and Chari are now married and have children of their own. The girls are doing well, seeing their mother often.

Mary Ruth's daughter, Chari, tried to develop a relationship with her father in the late 1980s. Charlie Jr. was living nearby in La Coste, Texas. Chari had never met her father, and arranged to visit him and his live-in girlfriend. Over the next few months, Chari got together with her father a few times in La Coste. Chari also invited Charlie and his girl friend to her home. During one visit to her father's home, money was taken from her purse, but Chari did not tell her father money was missing. Chari called her mother and told her about the missing money. Mary Ruth reminded Chari that she was against her seeing her dad from the outset. Mary Ruth reminded Chari that her father was never around for her. It was Mary Ruth's opinion that her father never cared about his girls. Chari was stubborn and said she just wanted to get to know her dad. Chari decided to keep seeing him.

During one visit, Charlie's girlfriend told Chari that Charlie, her father, said she was trying to sleep with him. Chari was devastated when she was told this by her father's girl friend. She never returned to her father's home—never seeing him again. In early 1998, Beth received a call from Charlie's sister Jeanette. Charlie Junior was dying from colon cancer. Beth felt she should pay her respects and asked her mother, Mary Ruth, to drive with her to Medina County. She wanted to visit her father one last time and say goodbye. When they got to San Antonio, Beth dropped Mary Ruth off at a restaurant. Mary Ruth was keeping an eye on Beth's children while she drove to Charlie's trailer in Natalia.

By now, Charlie Junior had another woman, named Dolly, living with him. Beth met Dolly at the door and she let her inside the mobile home to see Charlie. Beth was only gone an hour or two before she returned to San Antonio. She told Mary Ruth that her dad looked real bad, weighing about 70 pounds and was very pale. Charlie Junior needed oxygen to breathe. Beth was sad her father was dying, even though Charlie had never been there for her. Beth told Mary Ruth that her father wanted to see Mary Ruth one last time. Mary Ruth was hesitant, but decided to drive to Charlie's trailer. When she saw him, it was clear Charlie Junior was going to die soon. He looked very bad. He seemed to recognize Mary Ruth, but said little. Mary Ruth did not stay long, as it was hard to look at Charlie Junior in his condition. Charlie died a few days later. Mary Ruth did not attend his funeral, and neither did Chari, who was still mortified over what had happened. Beth however, decided to go to the services. Charlie's sisters and Beth were the only immediate family members at the funeral. This was especially sad since there are still many of the Hitzfelder family still residing in the San Antonio area.

Sheriff Charlie and Iona Leave This World

After Sheriff Charlie was voted out of office, not much is known about how he spent his final years. He passed away on May 4, 1993. He was 82 years old. At the time of his death, he was living in a care home just outside of Devine, Texas. He required 24 hours medical care. It is known that in the late 1980's Sheriff Charlie worked for a time as a security guard for a private security company. He was assigned to watch over the old Army Air field—also known as the Hondo Airport. This step down in status must have been hard for the old sheriff, especially after his 24 years of tremendous power as the county sheriff.

Iona Langford Hitzfelder passed on February 11, 1991.

EIGHT
How to Talk to Men With Those Lying Eyes

After Mary Ruth returned to Texas, Charlie Jr. remained in San Diego for a few months until he received his orders to report onboard the USS Ranger CV-61. The Ranger was a frontline Nimitz class aircraft carrier. The carrier was home ported at the Naval base in Alameda, California. When Charlie arrived in Alameda, he reported to the ship and was assigned a bunk. Charlie Junior was assigned as a clerk's assistant. The job was menial, requiring little effort, which was fine with Charlie. Naval fitness reports reveal that Charlie was a poor sailor and considered lazy.

Soon after beginning his new job, it became clear to the Navy that even this low-key job was going to be hard for Seaman Hitzfelder. He was often late for duty and failed to follow orders. He was AWOL on numerous occasions. A shipmate of Charlie's helped piece together his time aboard the USS Ranger. The sailor asked that his name be withheld. Charlie was assigned to the Second Division and held the rank of E-3 seaman.

The shipmate said that Charlie real interest was in the enlisted men's club on base, named the "Peppermint Lounge". The daughters of Navy personnel and girls from town were able to gain entry to the club. All they needed was a Navy Dependent ID card or a friend's Navy Dependent ID card.

Management never checked to see if the cards were legitimate; the lounge was only interested in keeping sailors happy. Girls dancing with sailors kept them buying drinks. There was no enforcement of drinking-age requirements. The Navy was willing to overlook a girl's age if she wanted entry into the club. Naval authorities saw no harm in this, as long as no one from the community or local law enforcement complained. Charlie loved the fact that young girls were in the club each afternoon after school. He considered these young girls easy targets. Many stayed late, until midnight or after. Some of the girls did not have parents keeping tabs on them. Their fathers were often away serving sea duty. Some of their mothers, who were also looking for companionship, accompanied a few of the young girls.

Charlie Junior also liked to visit the red light district of Alameda. Young prostitutes were everywhere, especially on or around payday. After several visits, Charlie set his sights on young prostitutes, the younger the better. Charlie Jr. gladly paid a premium to be with them. This pursuit became Charlie's lifetime obsession. Charlie Jr. liked rough, almost violent, sex. Some of the prostitutes specialized in this form of sex.

When Charlie found a girl he liked, he would settle into a sort of trance. All of his insecurities faded away, as if he was finally in control of his life and destiny. Charlie spent many nights and weekends with the prostitutes.

In April 1962, after being stationed on the Ranger for only one month, Charlie Jr. met a twelve-year-old girl at the Peppermill Lounge. Her name was Sandra Marie Moorefield. She was pretty and petite with long brown hair. At twelve, she was already shapely, attracting much attention from the sailors at the Peppermill. Sandra often dated sailors on shore leave. Sailors bought her meals, offered her alcohol, and often ended up having sex with her. Alameda investigators learned that she started having sex with older men when she was only eleven. Her first encounter was with a relative, her mother's brother. Sandra was also looking for a way out of her situation. Sandra lived with her mother on Gibbs Avenue in Alameda. Sandra's mother was a single parent and worked at the Hershey chocolate factory in the nearby town of San Leandro. Sandra's mother and father were alcoholics. After work, Sandra's mother would return home and begin drinking. She hardly ever cooked meals for Sandra, who had to fend on her own. By late afternoon, Sandra's mother usually passed out on the couch, freeing Sandra to sneak off to the Peppermill Lounge. Although not a service dependent, Sandra endeared herself to the management after several guest visits and would just show up and walk into the bar. The civilian bartenders who knew Sandra were aware that Sandra helped them make fast money in tips when the sailors danced with her.

Charlie Junior met Sandra one night while talking to a bartender, learning she was a regular patron. He asked Sandra for a dance, bought her a beer, and discovered she was only twelve. This pleased him immensely, immediately recognizing Sandra's vulnerability. Like a shark hunting prey, Charlie Jr. zeroed in Sandra, finding her easygoing, while he was cautious.

Prior to Sandra, Charlie Junior's sexual liaisons had been confined to young girls, like Carolyn and Mary Ruth. He had encountered a few younger prostitutes while in the Navy. Charlie Junior knew that Sandra was not a prostitute, just a young, lonely girl. She went to the club to get out of the house and escape the reality of her life. Charlie Jr. decided to move slowly with Sandra. Over the next few weeks, he offered to buy drinks and food for Sandra, befriending her. Charlie turned on what charm he could muster, making her feel that he was really a nice guy. This approach worked as Sandra gave Charlie her address. She lived in a triplex unit at 245-C Gibbs Avenue. She told Charlie that she babysat almost every Saturday night at 245-A Gibbs Avenue, Alameda, CA. This was two doors down from her house. Charlie Junior continued to lavish drinks, food, and small amounts of cash on Sandra when he could.

One Saturday night in early May 1962, Charlie Junior went into town to visit Sandra. Charlie was aware that Sandra was babysitting the young children of Vivian Sills. Charlie showed up at the home at around 10 PM, knowing the two babies would be asleep. He knocked on the door and was let in by Sandra. He brought in a six-pack of beer and some marijuana.

The children were in one of bedrooms, fast asleep. Charlie sat down on the large couch next to Sandra and offered her a beer. She took the beer and got up from the couch to turn off the television and turn on the radio. She returned to the couch as Charlie was rolling a marijuana cigarette. He lit the joint and offered it to Sandra. She took the joint, took a puff, returned it to Charlie, and drank her beer. The two sat on the couch for the next twenty minutes making small talk, drinking beer, and smoking marijuana.

A 1963 Alameda police report would later shed light on what happened next.

Charlie asked Sandra to have intercourse, but she refused at first. Charlie kept on insisting and she finally gave in. They had sex on the couch. Charlie did not use protection. Sandra didn't believe Charlie ejaculated. He told her he knew he could get into trouble for having sex with a minor and told her not to say anything to anyone about this. The official police report said that Sandra also told the police of a second act of intercourse with Charlie on November 7, 1962. Sandra was certain of the date, as it was two weeks before her thirteenth birthday. This second sexual encounter occurred at the home of Mrs. Wanda Meyers, who lived at 2019 B Pope Street in Alameda. Sandra was at the house visiting her friend, Betty Meyers. Mrs. Meyers was not home this night. Charlie saw Sandra at the Peppermill Lounge the night before and knew she would be at the Meyer home. He arrived around 9 P.M. Charlie took her to a bedroom and had sexual intercourse with her. Charlie did not use a condom and did not ejaculate during intercourse. She said the act was consensual.

On November 9, 1962, two days after Charlie's second sexual encounter with Sandra, the USS Ranger sailed for a six-month tour. The ship saw no action but patrolled the seas off Vietnam as a deterrent to rising tensions with Vietnam. Charlie continued to work as a clerk's assistant while aboard the USS Ranger. Charlie was a terrible sailor and did a lousy job. A commanding officer, in a personnel action, stated that Seaman Hitzfelder knew his job, but was either lazy or chose to do a bad job. He did not recommend Charlie for reenlistment in the Navy.

The time went by slowly for Charlie Junior. He reported to work each day, but rarely associated with other sailors. He never wrote to his parents and had no contact with them. Official Navy records report that Seaman Hitzfelder was treated medically for a sexually transmitted disease after a port call in Japan.

On June 14, 1963, the USS Ranger returned to Alameda and its sailors were given liberty. Charlie stayed in Alameda, resuming his daily routine of going to the Peppermill Lounge. When Charlie first visited the lounge, he learned that Sandra had been taken away to a camp for wayward girls. This did not worry him, but it did frustrate him having one less young girl available for his wants and needs. Three days after returning to port, Charlie was awakened in his shipboard bunk by two Shore Patrol officers. He was told he was under arrest for the rape of Sandra Moorefield.

The Long Arm of the Law Reaches for Miles

As Charlie was led from his bunk through the maze of corridors inside the USS Ranger, he was confused. He asked over and over why he was under arrest. The shore patrolmen told Charlie that civilian authorities had a warrant for his arrest. After reaching the main deck of the carrier, Charlie was led down the long gangplank to waiting Alameda police detectives. As the three men reached the detectives, Charlie, in a little boy's voice, questioned his arrest again. He wanted to know what he had done as he had been in the Far East for six months.

Detective Johnson of the Alameda Police told Charlie he was being arrested for raping a twelve-year-old girl. Charlie began to protest he was innocent. Detective Johnson asked Charlie if he knew a girl named Sandra Moorefield. As soon as Charlie heard the name, he blurted out that Sandra told him that she was sixteen. The detective repeated to Charlie that Sandra was only twelve years old when he took advantage of her. Charlie was scared as hell and knew he was in deep trouble. In 1963, having sex with a twelve-year-old girl meant serious jail time. Charlie tried to impress Detective Johnson by saying his father was a sheriff in Texas. Unfazed, the detective assured Charlie that his father's position in Texas would not help him in California. As handcuffs were applied, Charlie realized he was in real trouble. He was placed in the back seat of the waiting police car.

Charlie began to cry, sobbing like a baby. Tears rolled down his face as they drove away from the Ranger, through the Naval

Air Station. The police car made its way into town to the city jail. By now, Charlie had somewhat composed himself and asked when he would get a phone call. He was told that after he was booked he would be allowed to call anyone he wanted. Charlie was taken to the booking area, where he was photographed and fingerprinted. Charlie's property consisted of a yellow metal ring, a wristwatch, cigarettes and a lighter, a kit with toothbrush and toothpaste, and thirty-seven cents. Charlie was taken to a small room and told that he could make his phone call before being questioned. He dialed his mother and father's home phone number. After a few rings, Iona answered the phone. He told his mother he was in big trouble. Iona told Charlie Jr. to calm down and asked what was wrong. He told his mother he was in jail. Iona was furious, asking how he could get into this kind of mess. He told her that he was being charged with rape. Iona lost her composure, and screamed at Junior. She asked what he meant. Charlie Jr. told her that he was seeing a young girl who lied about her age. He told Iona that he did not know she was only twelve. Iona realized Charlie Jr. might be able to get away with such a thing in Texas, but that he was in very serious trouble. Iona was aware Charlie Jr. was dating a woman named Charlene and asked him if Charlene knew about his arrest. Charlie Jr. said she knew nothing about it. Charlie Jr. told his mother that this all happened before he met Charlene. Iona told her son to not say a word to anyone about anything. No matter what they say to him, he was to keep his mouth shut. The sheriff would take care of this.

Charlie Jr. thanked his mother for helping out and told her he would do as he was told. He would not say a word to the police. Iona told him to not thank her, but to thank his father when he got there. She told Charlie Jr., "Look at the mess you have gotten all of us into." Iona ended the call saying, "You damn well better keep your mouth shut." She slammed down the telephone receiver. Charlie hung up the phone. He must have thought to himself, "I sure hope my dad can get me out of this mess." Detective Johnson approached Charlie and took him to the interview room. He told Charlie he wanted to interview him about the charges against him. Charlie kept his word and said nothing. He reminded Johnson that his dad was a sheriff in Texas, and would come to California to get him out of this trouble. Still unimpressed, Johnson told Charlie he was going to need help. Once again Johnson asked Charlie to consider talking him. Charlie refused, which angered Detective Johnson. He was not used to suspects refusing to talk. In 1963, the Miranda warning, requiring police officers to inform a suspect his constitutional rights to stay silent, was not yet law. Police officers often intimidated suspects into giving a confession. Johnson was considering some sort of physical intimidation to get a confession, but thought Charlie's father might be a big shot and this could cause him some grief. Johnson decided against pushing Charlie into confessing and took him from the phone room back to a jail cell. Johnson opened the door and told Charlie there would be no bail for this charge. That meant Charlie could remain in jail until a trial or the court made some other determination. The cell door slammed loudly.

Charlie Jr., alone in his cell, began to cry again. Johnson commented to other jailers what a baby Charlie was. It was clear Charlie would never be able to do hard jail time. After the cell door slammed shut, the minutes and hours drug on and soon it was nightfall. One day came and went, then two, and finally the third day dawned. By the third day, Charlie was in a state of panic. He had not heard from anyone, including his father, the sheriff.

Around mid-morning, a jailer came to Charlie's cell and told him that he had visitors. Charlie was taken to a private room and not the normal inmate visiting room. As the door opened, Charlie looked inside and saw his dad. Texas Ranger Levy Duncan accompanied the sheriff. The men were sitting next to one another at a small desk. Both were decked out in the customary Stetson hats, boots, and western pants. Charlie Jr. could see the sheriff was angry. Pointing to the only other chair in the room, the sheriff commanded his son to sit down. Charlie Jr. was scared but relieved. He knew that his dad was mad as hell, but would get him out of the mess for the sake of his reputation as a Texas sheriff. Charlie was told to sit there and keep his mouth shut. His father said that he would do all the talking. Charlie Jr. obliged and did not speak. The sheriff said that he hoped Charlie had listened to his mother and not spoken to anyone. He assured his father that he had admitted nothing to the police officers. This seemed to relieve the sheriff, believing he may be able to get his son out of this mess. Sheriff Charlie asked him how he could get involved with such a young girl. Charlie Jr. lied and said he did not know Sandra's was only twelve. The sheriff was not buying Junior's explanation and told him straight out he was lying. Then, without a breath in between, the sheriff told his son he was happy he was lying. The lie may help him get out of this mess. Levy Duncan remained seated in his chair, never saying a word. Within a few minutes, the sheriff was done talking to his son. He told him to go back to his cell. As he left the room, he reminded Charlie Jr. to keep his mouth shut. He told his son that he would be back soon to get him out of the jail. Sheriff Charlie got up from his chair and walked right past Junior, opening the door and calling to the jailer to take his son back to jail.

The jailer walked up to Junior and took him by the arm, leading him down the hallway and back to his cell. As the sheriff and the ranger left the jail, Sheriff Charlie asked one of the jailers where he could find the Alameda County Sheriff. Sheriff Charlie was told he was in Oakland at the main offices. Ranger Duncan and Sheriff Charlie were driven to the Oakland offices of the Alameda County Sheriff. They were escorted to the private offices of the sheriff. No one knows for sure what happened during that meeting. Sheriff Charlie and Ranger Duncan were driven back to the jail in Alameda. When they arrived, they were told Charlie Jr. was being processed for release without having to post any bail. A release in a matter as serious as this was quite an accomplishment, even back in those days. The Alameda Sheriff bypassed normal bail procedures and allowed Charlie to be released. In about ten minutes, Charlie was led out of jail, where Sheriff Charlie and Ranger Duncan were waiting for him. As Junior walked up to his father, he thanked the sheriff for helping him out. His father replied that he was not helping Junior, he was helping himself. He told Junior that he was not going to let Junior ruin his career. Sheriff Charlie pointed to the car that had been arranged for them by the Alameda County Sheriff. He told Junior to get in the car and asked him for directions to the Naval base. Junior obliged and directed his father to the main gate. When they reached the main gate, Sheriff Charlie unceremoniously told Junior to get out of the car and report back to his ship.

And He Fixes Things That Can't Be Fixed

Sheriff Charlie and Ranger Duncan discussed strategy together after they dropped off Charlie at the Naval base. The sheriff asked Duncan to find the district attorney's office on the map. Ranger Duncan found the address, and as they drove he gave the sheriff directions. About twenty minutes later, they arrived at the Alameda County District Attorney's office in downtown Oakland. Sheriff Charlie parked in front of the building. He parked in an area restricted to lawyers, judges, and other officials. Ranger Duncan commented that maybe they should not park there. Sheriff Charlie ignored Duncan's suggestion and parked anyway. They walked into the main lobby of the District Attorney's office. As they entered the district attorney's outer office, Charlie told Ranger Duncan to do what he was there to do. Duncan said he would handle the district attorney. Duncan and the sheriff walked to the reception area.

As they approached the secretary, Duncan announced that he was a Texas Ranger and was there on official business to see the district attorney. He pointed at Sheriff Charlie and said that the man with him was the sheriff of Medina County, Texas. The receptionist looked impressed as she eyed the ranger's circular star badge. She asked the men to have a seat and disappeared into a private office just off the main corridor. After a few minutes, she returned.

The secretary told the men that the district attorney's chief assistant would see them now. She said the district attorney was out of the office. Sheriff Charlie looked disappointed and said they wanted to see the head man. Charlie was told that they were seeing the district attorney's number one assistant. Sheriff Charlie commented that this would be okay, as long as he has the power to take care of his problem. Both men were escorted into the private office and introduced to Thomas Glenn. The men shook hands, and the door closed.

What happened next was no surprise to people familiar with how things were done in the 1960s. People with political connections, Hollywood stars, and the wealthy got special accommodations from some prosecutors. Back in the 1960s, the term, "Money talks and bullshit walks" was common. Politics and good old boy connections worked back then, and to a certain extent, work today. After only ten or fifteen minutes, District Attorney Glenn escorted Sheriff Charlie and Ranger Duncan from the private office. All three had smiles on their faces as they walked to the front steps of the building. The sheriff was told to not worry about a thing, that all would be taken care of. Both Duncan and the sheriff shook hands with District Attorney Glen. Sheriff Charlie told Glen to bring his family to Medina County and they would do the town. Sheriff Charlie and Ranger Duncan drove back to the county offices in Oakland and met with the deputy sheriff who had set up the transportation and made introductions on their behalf. Sheriff Charlie and the ranger were driven to the San Francisco Airport. About two hours later, they boarded a commercial airliner to San Antonio.

And Justice For All

In July 1963, Charlie Jr. received a letter from the Alameda County Probation Department. He was asked to report for an interview. When he showed up for his pre-sentence probation report he was met by Probation Officer C. Daniel Estorga. Charlie was interviewed for about one hour. He answered all of Mr. Estorga's questions politely. This was all he needed to do. Charlie Jr. was very happy. He knew that a good outcome had been arranged. He thanked the probation officer and left.

In August 1963, Charlie Junior received a second letter from the Alameda County District Attorney. Charlie learned that the felony charge of rape had been reduced to the misdemeanor charge of contributing to the delinquency of a minor. Charlie learned that he would be sentenced to 90 days in jail, of which 60 days were suspended. He would also receive one year informal probation. He was ordered to stay away from girls under eighteen for the length of his probation. He was told that his conviction would be expunged after successfully completing probation. There was a notation in the probation report stating Charlie Jr. would receive only a nominal probation period. Probation was to serve as an additional reminder of the seriousness of this matter, after probation he would qualify for a timely clearing of his record. There was a mention that Charlie wanted to go into law enforcement like his father, a county sheriff in Texas. The way the official probation report was written as well as the light sentence Charlie Junior received was a testament to Sheriff Charlie's political influence. Sheriff Charlie was able to wield his influence thousands of miles from home.

On August 19, 1963, Charlie Junior showed up at the Alameda County Sheriff's Department to serve thirty days in jail. Charlie was taken to the downtown jail by sheriff deputies and booked. He would only serve twenty-six days in jail before being released. Charlie Junior was given credit for his four days in jail when arrested. On September 12, 1963, he was released from jail and returned to duty aboard the USS Ranger.

Charlie's remaining time in the Navy was remarkable only for his continued incompetence in performing his duties as a clerk. He often received reprimands for his lack of attention to duty and was cited for being AWOL for a few hours on three occasions. He stayed close to the ship and rarely ventured back to the Peppermill Lounge. It was clear to Charlie junior that another brush with the law during his probation period may bring him serious jail time.

Charlie Junior did not like being in jail. While serving the remainder of the thirty-day sentence, he was exposed to some hard-core criminals. These men frightened him. He had never been in a fight with a man in his life. He feared that some of the tougher inmates would hurt him. During his brief stay in jail, he stayed in his cell as much as he could. He did not make eye contact with the inmates around him and spoke to no one.

Charlie Junior would have one more serious brush with Naval authorities. The USS Ranger was scheduled for a week-long training cruise. The Vietnam War was just ramping up and the USS Ranger was being readied for deployment. Most of the crew received liberty up until 6 AM Charlie Junior took this opportunity to go into town as many sailors did. His alcoholism was now blossoming, and would continue to play a significant role in the remainder his life.

On this night, Charlie got extremely drunk and was driving around town looking for a prostitute. While waiting in a parking lot for a girl, Charlie passed out. He woke up around 7 AM When he regained his senses; he realized he was late reporting for duty. He drove as fast as he could back to the base. As he entered the main gate, he was told that the USS Ranger had already departed. Charlie told the guards at the gate that he was supposed to be onboard the Ranger. The Shore Patrol promptly arrested Charlie. They drove his car to the long-term parking area reserved for sailors on sea duty. Charlie Jr. was taken to the Treasure Island brig and locked up. He was now looking at some serious jail time. The U.S. was now involved in the Vietnam conflict and Charlie Jr. was AWOL from the warship. As before, Charlie was allowed a telephone call. Charlie Jr. called his father and told him he was in trouble again. The sheriff responded angrily, asking what he had done now. Charlie Jr. told his father that he missed the Ranger's sailing. Sheriff Charlie was not surprised. Charlie Jr. warned his father that this could mean he could be put on trial as a war deserter. The sheriff told him that was not going to happen as long as he was still sheriff. He told his son to hang up the phone and to not worry. The sheriff was going to get him out of trouble once again. Charlie was returned to his cell.

The next day, Chief Petty Officer Washington came to Charlie's cell. He told him that he was going to be released. Washington said the Navy was going to list his absence as unavoidable and excused. He commented to Charlie that he must have some connections. Sheriff Charlie's influence reached all the way to the upper echelons of the Navy. Once again, Charlie Sr. managed to save his son from trouble with the law.

Charlie was released from the brig and told to report for duty to a supply unit at the Alameda Naval Air Station. The remainder of Charlie's service time, about six months, was spent at this supply unit. Charlie was assigned quarters on the grounds of the navy base. After work, Charlie Jr. would drink until he was totally intoxicated. On several occasions, he would show up to duty a few minutes or few hours late hung over. Even after all of the trouble he had been in, Charlie would venture into town searching for young girls, occasionally finding one.

Charlie was beginning to be known by "working girls" for his reputation of rough treatment. The prostitutes learned to ask Charlie for a premium for their services. Charlie did not venture anywhere else to meet young girls, fearing he would be arrested. He confined his sexual escapades to professionals, knowing that it would be safer for him. He did not want to have contact with law enforcement.

Charlie's poor performance on duty caused him to be written up by his superiors on several occasions. However, he never received formal punishment. On occasion, he received extra duty for disobeying orders. Charlie completed active duty on November 13, 1964. He was assigned to inactive status in the Naval Reserve. Two years later he received a general discharge under honorable conditions. Even though Charlie had expressed his desire to go into law enforcement, he never entered this career field. He did not immediately return to Texas, staying in California until 1971. Charlie's relationship with his father and mother remained strained. Before getting out of the Navy, he met a young woman named Charlene, who lived in Sacramento. After getting out of the service, Charlie moved to Sacramento, where he found work as a gas station attendant. He moved to a small house located at 1514½ 23rd Street in Sacramento, California.

NINE
"A Mean and Nasty Man"

Charlene was married to Charlie Jr. from July 13, 1964 to February 24, 1971. Charlie met this sixteen-year-old girl when he was stationed aboard the USS Ranger. Early in 1962 Charlie and some shipmates would drive to the Sacramento area on weekends to visit their girlfriends. At first, Charlie was not dating any of these girls, but eventually struck up a conversation with his future wife while on one of his weekend visits. Charlie's ex-wife is semi-retired now, living in a town in Northern California. She was very cooperative and accommodating in the development of this book. She asked to have her name changed for reasons of privacy. Charlie married Charlene on July 13, 1964. When Charlie first met Charlene, she was dating a sailor Charlie knew. Charlie and his buddies would drive up to Folsom, outside of Sacramento, not far from the Alameda NAS. The drive was about two hours.

Charlene said Charlie was a handsome young man, and that he swept her off her feet. They began to exchange letters. Charlene lived in Folsom and attended Folsom High School.

Charlene said that at the beginning of their romance, Charlie was the perfect gentleman. Her mother also thought Charlie was a nice guy. Charlene's mother used to lend Charlie money for gasoline to come and go to Folsom. He never paid her back. After exchanging letters and having several dates in the Sacramento area, Charlie asked Charlene to marry him. Charlene's mother was skeptical of Charlie's family life in Texas. To make Charlene's mother feel better about his upbringing, Charlie asked Charlene and her mother to go to Texas to meet his family.

Charlene and her mother drove to Hondo to meet Charlie's

parents, Iona and Charlie Sr. They drove to Hondo alone, leaving Charlie aboard the USS Ranger. Upon arriving in Hondo, Charlene said she was impressed with Charlie's parents. Charlie's mother, Iona, was described as a very pretty woman. She seemed very protective and loving of her son. Charlene said that Charlie's father seemed like a nice man. Even at sixteen, Charlene knew instantly that the sheriff was a very powerful man in Texas. After a few days, Charlene and her mother decided that Charlie's family was a good family. Charlene's mother declared Charlie Jr. to be the good man he portrayed himself to be. Charlene called Charlie back in California and agreed to marry him.

The next day, the sheriff took Charlene and her mother to San Antonio to buy a diamond engagement ring. They went to a Zale's, where she picked out a beautiful ring, which was paid for by Charlie's father. As if seeing the future, Charlie's father took Charlene aside and told her that if anything ever happened between them, he wanted her to promise to return the ring. Charlene promised to do so.

While in Texas, Charlene and her mother met Charlie's sisters, Jeanette and Barbara.

She really liked his sisters. They were nice to her. Many years later, Jeanette called her to tell her that Charlie had passed away.

On November 9, 1962, before they were married, Charlie and the USS Ranger were deployed for a six-month tour of Vietnam. Charlene was still attending high school in Folsom. The Ranger returned to Alameda NAS on June 7, 1963.

While Charlie was onboard the Ranger, Charlene wrote him almost daily. During the time Charlie Jr. was away, she received few letters from Charlie. One card came when he was on leave in Japan. Charlene remembered that the postmark was from Japan. She also remembered that Charlie wrote he got "an infection" while overseas. Charlene did not know that Charlie's infection was a sexually transmitted disease from a Japanese prostitute.

A year or so after they got married, Charlie Jr. was talking to a man they both knew when he blurted out that he got a dose of the clap in Japan. Charlene remembered Charlie Jr. said he had an "infection" when he was in Japan. She finally figured out that he must have had sex with a prostitute. If she had known this at the time, it would have made a big difference to her.

After being back from Japan for only a few days, Charlie was arrested by civilian authorities for the rape of Sandra Moorefield. Charlie Jr. told Charlene that he had some trouble with the law, but she never knew that he had been arrested for raping a girl. Charlene was still living in Folsom with her parents. Charlene learned of Charlie's arrest when he called her as he was being booked. He told her he had been arrested over owing someone money.

Before Charlie's discharge from the Navy, he took a weekend liberty. Charlene and Charlie drove to Reno, Nevada. They where were married on July 13, 1964. Charlene only learned decades later that Charlie had been arrested for rape. She said that if she had known Charlie Jr. had raped a girl, she would have never married him. After the civil ceremony Charlene returned to live with her mother. She planned to stay with her mother and continue high school until Charlie's discharge from the Navy on November 13, 1964. Charlene and Charlie continued seeing one another on weekends, whenever Charlie got liberty.

After Charlie was discharged, the couple rented a basement apartment on Main Street in Orangevale, California. Charlie got a job working as an attendant at a Shell gasoline station. Charlene continued her high school education. After graduation, she found a civil service job. After her marriage ended, she continued to work at this job for many years.

Charlie worked at the gasoline station for less than two months, accepting a new job at Van Alsteins. He did not stay at that job very long either, going to work for B.M.D., located on Roseville Road in North Highlands. Charlene remembers that job involved construction work. Charlene and Charlie moved several times during their marriage. They first moved to Sacramento and then to Rancho Cordova, where they lived in a duplex.

To others, their marriage appeared successful, but Charlene confided that Charlie would often beat her with his fists. He was a brutal man. During one beating, Charlie knocked out one of her teeth. One day she hid from him behind a freezer with her little dog. The dog did not make a sound or Charlie would have beaten them both. Charlene never told her mother that Charlie was such a brutal man. She was young and not yet wise to the ways of the world. Back then, she thought the way he treated her was how marriage worked.

Charlene recalled one incident where she feared for her life. On this occasion, Charlie was angry with her. They were arguing over money as they often did. Charlie Jr. got his gun and he pointed it at her head. He said that if she did not listen to him, he would kill her. She really thought he would when he pointed the gun at the back of her head and said, "Two bullets in the back of the head will do it every time." She did not have the courage or strength to leave him.

Charlie would often hang out at beer joints, leaving her home, as she was too young to go with him. She spent a lot of time alone. Charlie came home drunk and demand sex from her. He controlled the money, and did a really bad job at it. Charlene stayed with Charlie out of fear. He threatened to hunt her down and kill her if she ever left him. Charlene was positive that Charlie's threats were sincere.

Charlene knew of Charlie's two little girls from his marriage to Mary Ruth. During the five years they were together, the girls never came to visit. Charlie once talked about his daughters coming to visit, but they never did. Charlene did not recall if Charlie ever telephoned his girls or if they ever called him. She did not remember any letters coming to the house from either Mary Ruth or the girls.

During their marriage Charlie and Charlene visited Hondo together one time. Charlene's second visit to Texas came when Charlie's grandmother died. While in Hondo, Charlie, the sheriff, and Charlene transported a prisoner to Gainesville, Texas. She recalled the long drive in the sheriff's car.

When Charlene and Charlie lived in a duplex on De Soto Way in Ranch Cordova, Charlene became best friends with Cindy, a girl living on the other side of the duplex. Cindy's cousin, Melanie Holksey, often came to visit. Melanie was from Ohio before moving to California.

Charlene and Charlie's marriage finally ended when Charlene learned Charlie was having affairs with other women. She discovered he had a girlfriend in Meadow Vista and another in Washington State. Charlene also suspected Charlie was having an affair with Melanie, but did not say anything at first. In November 1969, she was looking through Charlie's personal things and found a little black book with the names of girls Charlie had been seeing. This was the last straw. Charlene finally drew the courage to tell Charlie she wanted a divorce. Charlie laughed at her, which was a surprise, because in the past he had threatened to kill her. Charlie did not refuse the divorce and did not make a scene. In reflection, she decided he was ready to leave her for Melanie.

After they decided to separate, Charlie helped her move from the duplex to a house she rented in Sacramento. After leaving Charlie Jr., Charlene did not have any further problems with him. She suspected this was because her brother was a deputy sheriff and that Charlie knew her brother drove by her house to check on her. She also believed her brother had police friends drive by to keep an eye on the house. At night, she would occasionally see a police car's spotlight illuminate the front windows of her house. Joint property was divided at the time of the divorce. Charlie kept his 1967 Oldsmobile Cutlass, while Charlene kept her 1961 Hillman. To this day, Charlene has not told her mother that Charlie would beat her. She was embarrassed being married to a man like Charlie. Charlene felt that if her family knew of Charlie's violent behavior, they would have done something bad to Charlie. One of the best days of her life was when the divorce was finalized. Charlene later learned that Charlie married Melanie and moved to Texas in 1971. She never saw Charlie again, and that was okay with Charlene.

Charlie's Third Marriage: Melanie Holksey "One Day Her Innocence Was Lost"

Before Charlie's divorce from Charlene in 1970, he had been

introduced to Melanie Holksey. Melanie was a cousin of Cindy Albaugh, who lived next door to Charlie and Charlene in Rancho Cordova, California. Melanie was twenty-one and the single mother of four-year-old Ellie Mae. Melanie was an attractive, vulnerable woman. Charlie stepped into this relationship and quickly took advantage of the situation. Melanie Holksey was fifty-two when she died of a brain aneurysm in Madisonville, Texas in 2003. Melanie's family believes to this day that repeated beatings and blows to her head, at the hands of Charlie, contributed to her death.

I spoke to Melanie's daughter Ellie Mae. Today, she is in her middle 40s with her own children and grandchildren. Ellie recounted what she termed the "hellish portion of her life." Ellie Mae's half-brother is Charles Joseph Hitzfelder III Charlie Junior's only son. Ellie Mae calls her brother "Buddy". Buddy was born in 1976.

Ellie Mae married at fifteen. She has two children from her first marriage, which ended in divorce because she married too young. Ellie Mae remarried and finally found happiness in her life. She works daily and helps out with her grandchildren. Ellie Mae enjoys a modest life in central Florida. She was only four when her mother met Charlie. Ellie Mae was only eleven or twelve when they divorced.

Charlie Jr. and his new family moved from California to Galveston, Texas in 1971. They chose Galveston because Melanie's parents lived in the Galveston area.

Over the years, the family moved to various house trailers and apartments around Galveston. They lived in Texas City, Dickenson, Arcadia, Santa Fe, Alvin, and Humble, Texas. Ellie Mae recalled the family living at the Atascocita Village Mobile Home Park in Humble. Ellie Mae recalled the address as 520 Atascocita Road, Space #16 Humble, Texas. Ellie Mae said that Charlie Jr. never had anyone visit him at the house. He was a loner for the most part. Charlie's personality was such that Ellie Mae's school friends would not come around the house. They did not like Charlie, because he was mean to them when they came over. They were afraid of the sinister look on Charlie's face. He would stare at her friends, making them feel uncomfortable.

When the family moved from California to Galveston, Charlie got a job working for a company called Can-Go Trucking. Charlie drove an eighteen-wheel truck. On occasion, Charlie would be out of town on three- or four-day runs. While he was gone Ellie Mae felt safe. Those were good times for Ellie Mae. Charlie lost his job as a truck driver after being arrested for drunk driving. Somehow he managed to stay employed at Can-Go, working as a dispatcher. Back then, Charlie drove a 1973 blue Pontiac hatchback. He would often take Ellie Mae with him around town, making her sit close to him. He would put his right hand on her thigh and play with her underpants as he drove.

Even as a little girl, Ellie Mae recalled Charlie had a severe drinking problem. He drank beer and Jack Daniel's whiskey almost daily. When he began to drink, he would not stop until he passed out or threw up in the toilet. When Charlie drank, he became meaner. His personality was generally offensive, but he grew even stranger when drinking. Charlie would wake up in the morning and ask what he did the previous night. He would ask if he went anywhere. He always seemed to forget that he hit Melanie or Ellie Mae. As soon as Charlie woke up in the morning, he would grab a beer from the refrigerator and start drinking again, while he chain-smoked cigarettes.

When Ellie Mae was twelve, she had shoulder-length, blond hair, blue eyes, and stood 5'8" tall. When her Melanie was twenty-one, she had blond-colored hair and usually kept it shoulder length. She had brown eyes and a nice figure. People always remarked that she was very pretty.

Ellie Mae's recollections of her life with Charlie Jr. are stunningly graphic. Her memories chronicle child abuse, spousal abuse, rape, and brutality. Ellie Mae said she endured molestations and rape at the hands of Charlie Junior beginning at a very young age. She described her life as a living hell throughout her mother's marriage to Charlie Jr. She remembers that Charlie would beat her mother, almost daily. He would also beat her, often for little or no reason.

Ellie Mae remembered that when she was only 7 or 8 years

old, her mom would let her drive around town alone with Charlie. This frightened Ellie Mae. Charlie would always insist Ellie Mae dress up, as if she was older. When they drove around town, Charlie would make her sit close to him, almost like she was his girlfriend. As they drove around town, Charlie would place his hands on her thighs. This was only the beginning.

Ellie Mae recalls the sexual abuse she endured at the hands of Charlie Jr. began when she was about nine years old. Charlie was able get her to submit to his wishes by threats of violence. He would scare her and was able to control her by invoking fear of death upon her. Charlie would threaten to kill her mother and her grandfather if she did not do what he wanted. Charlie knew well that they were the ones closest to her and would use that love against her. After he started sexually abusing Ellie Mae, he often told her; "If you do not comply with my requests", I will kill your mama and grandpa ". He often said, "Remember, do as I say or you too will die." Ellie Mae was scared to death of Charlie, robbing her of sleep for years even after her mother divorced Charlie.

Ellie Mae said that Charlie's pattern to sexually abuse her was always similar. She remembered he would wait until her mother left the house before taking her into his bedroom. Charlie started his abuse by making her to massage him. Soon, after the massages began, Charlie would take her hand and put it on his penis. She remembered that Charlie taught her to masturbate him. Soon, he started performing sex upon Ellie Mae with his fingers. After a few months, Charlie made her have intercourse with him. Charlie told her little girls were made to please their step-dads. She knew Charlie was not supposed to do such things to her, but she was terrified of him and could not tell her mother about the abuse. Charlie and Melanie were married for five years. Ellie Mae said it seemed like fifty.

The sexual abuse ended in 1973. The family was living in a mobile home in Humble, Texas. Ellie Mae was ten. One evening, Ellie Mae's mother went to a friend's house, leaving her alone with Charlie. Ellie Mae knew the abuse would follow. But she said nothing. As soon as her mother walked out the door, Charlie took her by the arm and walked her over to a chair in the front room of the trailer. He told her to get down on her knees. Charlie unbuckled his jeans and pulled his pants and underwear down. She knew that he wanted her to perform oral sex on him again. He grabbed his penis and told her to put it in her mouth. She was afraid, but this time she would not do what he asked. Charlie raised his voice and said he was going to kill her mother and grandpa. Then Charlie told her he would shoot her in her head.

As Charlie was making his threats, Ellie Mae's mom suddenly opened the trailer door. Ellie Mae was still down on her knees. When Melanie came in, she saw Charlie pulling up his pants. Melanie's face turned white. She screamed at Charlie, demanding to know what was going on. Charlie told Melanie that Ellie Mae was being bad, and he was going to take his belt off and spank her. Melanie yelled at Ellie Mae, telling her to go to the kitchen. Ellie Mae did what she was told. Ellie Mae stood at the kitchen sink, doing dishes. Ellie Mae heard her mom and Charlie yelling at one another. Melanie left Charlie in the front room and looked into the kitchen. Pointing toward the door, she told Ellie Mae to run out the door as fast as she could. Melanie was just behind her. As they got to the bottom of the steps, Charlie was just behind and closing on them. Just a few feet outside, Ellie Mae's grandpa appeared and saw them running from Charlie. Her grandpa yelled out, "What the hell is going on here?" Melanie said hysterically to get into grandpa's car. Charlie looked up and saw grandpa coming toward him. Charlie immediately turned and ran back inside the trailer, locking the door. Ellie Mae's grandpa frantically tried to get into the trailer. He yelled at Charlie, "Open the door, you bastard!" Charlie refused. In spite of Ellie Mae's grandpa being an old man, Charlie was terrified of him. Melanie and Ellie Mae drove off with grandpa. Grandpa asked Ellie Mae if Charlie had ever touched her in an inappropriate way. She said he had and that it had been going on for a long time. At first, Melanie refused to believe Ellie Mae. She could not cope with the fact that she had been leaving Ellie Mae alone with Charlie. Ellie Mae's grandpa said that they were taking Ellie Mae to a hospital to confirm the molestation. Melanie was afraid to go to the hospital, fearing the truth. But Melanie finally realized the abuse could not continue and all three drove to Herman Hospital in Houston. The doctors told Melanie that Ellie Mae had been sexually assaulted in the past. Her grandpa was furious. Melanie started crying.

After that evening, Ellie Mae's memory becomes hazy. She recalled that a year or so later, they all went to court in Humble, Texas. Even then, Ellie Mae suspected her mother did not believe her. On the morning before the court hearing, Charlie Sr. and Iona came by the house. Iona asked Melanie to go for a drive with them. Sheriff Charlie was wearing his gun and hat. Melanie was intimidated, but agreed to go with them. They were only gone a few minutes. Ellie Mae recalled that her mother was very nervous, but said nothing.

Later that morning, Iona met Melanie and Ellie Mae outside the courtroom. Iona took Melanie by the hand and told her to sit beside her and Sheriff Charlie. Ellie Mae's grandparents sat on the other side of the court. Ellie Mae was upset and could not understand why her mother sat by Charlie's parents. Ellie Mae did not know her mother had endured threats that morning. Ellie Mae recalled Iona making hand gestures to her while she was on the witness stand. Iona acted like a loving grandmother, pretending she was waving to Ellie Mae. Even though she was only eleven, she knew that Iona was only trying to look like she cared about her. Ellie Mae knew better. Iona was often mean to her and it was apparent that she did not like Ellie Mae.

No one knows for sure what happened in court that day, but the charges against Charlie were dropped. When it was over, Charlie looked over at Ellie Mae, giving her a nasty look.

Many years later Ellie Mae learned that Sheriff Charlie took his gun out of his holster and pointed it Melanie's head that morning. Melanie told Ellie Mae that Charlie's dad said he would hunt her down and put two bullets in her head if his son was convicted. Ellie Mae learned that Charlie and Iona told her mother to sit with them in court and to smile at Charlie when he came into the courtroom. Ellie Mae is sure today that her mother was afraid of Sheriff Charlie and believed he would have killed them both. Shortly after the court hearing, for reasons Ellie Mae never understood, her mother went back to live with Charlie. Ellie Mae was very angry and afraid, but there was nothing she could do. After they resumed living with Charlie, he continued to beat Melanie almost daily, often giving her black eyes. After the day in court, Melanie never left Ellie Mae alone with Charlie, but he continued to yell and spank Ellie Mae. Her best recollection is that Charlie did not molest her after they went to court.

In May 1975, Melanie got pregnant with Ellie Mae's half-brother, Buddy. Charlie continued to beat her mom, even when she was pregnant. At times, Charlie would tell Melanie to leave him, and then abruptly threaten to kill them both if they left. In spite of all the abuse, Melanie never called the police on Charlie out of fear at what he might do. She was also terrified of what Sheriff Charlie could do. Melanie believed he could have her arrested or worse, killed.

Ellie Mae was afraid of Charlie Sr. and Iona. Ellie Mae recalled that before Charlie was caught molesting her, they drove to Hondo to visit Charlie's parents. Ellie Mae was in the front room watching television. She announced that she had to go to the bathroom. Iona said she would show Ellie Mae to the bathroom. Iona took her by the hand and walked her down the hallway. As they passed by a table with a vase on it, Iona took Ellie Mae's hand and knocked over the vase, breaking it. Iona went into the living room and told Charlie Jr., "Look what this bad little girl did." Charlie Jr. yelled at Ellie Mae and threatened her with a belt. He told her he was going to whip the tar out of her. Iona smiled as Charlie scolded her. Even as a little girl, Ellie Mae knew Iona was a mean lady.

When Melanie was six months pregnant, she and Charlie got into an argument. During the argument, Charlie told Melanie to get her daughter and her stuff, and get the hell out before he killed them both. Almost as soon as Charlie said this, he changed his tone and asked her to not leave him. Melanie was so afraid of Charlie she did not know what to do. Ellie Mae could not stand to be around Charlie anymore. She was fearful he would kill them both. Ellie Mae made a desperate plea to her mother, telling her she wanted to live with her grandparents if she did not leave Charlie.

This finally convinced Melanie to leave. The next morning, after Charlie went to work, Melanie called her friend Joe Franklin Scott for help. Joe came to their trailer and helped pack some of their belongings. Joe drove Melanie and Ellie Mae to Tyler, Texas. Ellie Mae felt that Joe was a nice man for helping them. Melanie was six months pregnant with Buddy, but this did not matter to Joe. He still helped them out. Melanie later married Joe, helping to raise Ellie Mae and Charlie III, or Buddy.

Ellie Mae does not remember ever again seeing Charlie after moving to Tyler. Buddy saw his father the first and only time as a teenager in the mid-1990s. Buddy had been asking what his real was dad like and where he lived. Buddy had questions about his life. Joe was the only father he had even known. Joe raised Buddy as if he was his own son. Buddy always called Joe his father. In response to Buddy's questions, Melanie and Joe decided to introduce him to his birth father. They arranged to drive into Houston to meet Charlie. Ellie Mae did not go along for the meeting, because of her fear of Charlie.

Buddy looked just like Charlie. On the day Buddy met his father, Melanie and Joe decided to tell Buddy that Charlie had molested Ellie Mae when she was young. Buddy was furious and said he should have killed Charlie. Buddy never saw Charlie again.

The Underpants Are Missing

On November 3, 1972, Charlie Junior reported a not-so-ordinary crime. The Galveston County Sheriff's Department received a telephone call from Charles J. Hitzfelder Jr. He wanted to report a burglary at his rented house on 2804 Shouse Road in Alta Loma. When a sheriff's deputy arrived at the Hitzfelder home Charlie Jr. met him. For the next ten minutes, Charlie Jr. told the deputy about the burglary of his house. Charlie showed the deputy three places inside his home with suspected blood stains. Charlie showed how the front door to his house had been pried open. Charlie said the only thing missing were the panties belonging to

Mrs. Hitzfelder and her daughter. Charlie went on to say that the large, white dog he owned might have bitten the intruder, scaring him away. Charlie could not explain how the intruder was able to locate the underpants belonging to Melanie and Ellie Mae if he was chased away by the dog. The sheriff did not collect physical evidence from the home, nor did he investigate any further. The burglary case was closed due to lack of evidence. The investigating officer wondered why someone would break into Charlie's house and only take underpants. At the time of this crime report, no one in the law enforcement thought to connect Charlie to the murders of several young girls in the area. Many of the victims had their underpants taken from the crime scene. Sometimes criminals subconsciously ask to be caught. Charlie's report could have been significant if further examined by the Texas Rangers. The Texas Rangers had questioned Charlie in 1971 when he relocated to Galveston County. The murders in the Galveston area had just begun. No one in law enforcement ever connect the dots.

Where's Charlie "Buddy" Hitzfelder?

Charlie's son, Charles Hitzfelder III, or Buddy as Ellie Mae calls him is living in Wiggins, Mississippi. There was no love lost between Buddy and his father, whom he referred to as "that sperm donor." Buddy said he never considered Charlie Jr. his father and thought of Joe Franklin as his father. Joe Franklin raised Buddy and Ellie Mae. He was always there for them. Buddy was aware of the many suspicions surrounding his birth father. He knew he beat women and had molested his sister. Buddy wished that he were older when he finally met his father. He was a teenager when he learned of the tragic abuse endured by Ellie Mae. He would have tried his best to beat his father. When he was around fifteen, he went with his mother and stepfather to Houston to pick up Joe's payroll check. They were living about one hour north of Houston at the time. Every two weeks, Joe would drive to Houston for his paycheck. Buddy and his mother always went with Joe and had lunch at the same restaurant in Houston.

They were at the restaurant one day when Charlie showed up. Buddy had already finished his hamburger and was playing a video game in the back of the restaurant. Melanie looked out the window and told him she would be right back. She walked outside and spoke to a man. That man came into the restaurant and Melanie introduced Buddy to his birth father. She suggested that the two should talk. Buddy agreed. Before this day, Buddy had always thought of Joe as his real dad. Charlie and Buddy went outside and sat on a bench to talk. Melanie and Joe stood a few feet away as they talked. Buddy recalls that Charlie played the part of a caring father. He acted as if he was interested in learning more about Buddy. Charlie told Buddy that he was driving truck and asked if Buddy wanted to go on a ride with him. Charlie asked him what kind of things he liked to do. Buddy told Charlie that he had been riding dirt bikes since he was five. Charlie promised to buy him a new motorbike. They talked for about ten minutes and Charlie said he would call him on the phone and arrange to take him on a trip on his truck. He mentioned a second time that he was going to buy Buddy a new motorcycle.

Charlie Hitzfelder never called Buddy and never saw his son again. In retrospect, Buddy believes that was a good thing. On the way home to Bedias, Texas, Melanie and Joe told Buddy what Charlie had done to Ellie Mae when she was a little girl. When he heard what had been done to Ellie Mae, he wanted to kill his father. Buddy learned that Charlie felt like a big man when hitting women. Buddy felt that his dad was a coward and would never stand up to a man.

A few years later, Buddy learned from one of Charlie's daughters that his father had died. The woman told Buddy she was his half sister. Until this phone call, Buddy never knew about his half sisters. Melanie never mentioned Charlie's other children. Buddy was told that Charlie died from cancer and he was asked to attend Charlie's funeral, but Buddy refused. Buddy told his half sister that Charlie was a no-good bastard. His half-sister was mad that Buddy would not attend the funeral. She asked him if he had any feelings for his father and Buddy replied that he did not.

Buddy has never had any contact with anyone in Charlie's family in Hondo. His first and only contact was the call from one of Charlie's daughters in the late 1990s. He didn't want to meet his family. They had never expressed an interest in him and he had no desire to meet any of them.

The Sheriff's Son

Lessons Learned

A CHILLING 20-PAGE PHOTOGRAPHIC RECORD
OF THE VICTIMS, THE KILLERS, THE EVIDENCE.

Wayne Skarka

Sheriff Donald "Butch" Campsey (1977)

Young "Butch" Campsey

Vote for Donald "Butch" Campsey for Sheriff

Sheriff Charlie Hitzfelder, Medina County Sheriff
1954-1977 (Official Photo From Sheriff's Office)

Iona, Charlie Junior and Sheriff Charlie Hitzfelder (Circa 1982)

Seaman
Charlie Hitzfelder
(Circa 1962)

Claudette Carolyn
Covey
(Circa 1960)

Site where Claudette's body was found.

Field where Claudette's body was found.

And a past that's dark and hazy,

with the words carved out in stone

Juanita Lamb's grave in Hitchcock, Texas

<u>(Note: Charles Jr. name)</u>

8-year-old
Ellie Mae Holskey

Melanie and
Ellie Mae Holskey
1985

Eva Sweet, Patricia Sweet, Charlie Hitzfelder Jr.,

Wesley Sweet and Frances Sweet (July 2, 1980)

Trailer in Natalia, Texas where Charlie Hitzfelder Jr. died

One of two headstones for Charles Hitzfelder Jr.

Some of the missing girls...

HARD AT ELDERLY
Col. 6

battle Tuesday
Page 1

The News

Monday
April 6, 1981
SAN ANTONIO, TEXAS
Street Final
25c

Link sought in slayings of 40 young Texas girls

ANGLETON (AP) — Investigators searched today for a missing link in the "sadistic" slayings of 40 young girls reported missing in southeast Texas during the past 10 years.

"There has got to be a common denominator in all the killings. We just haven't found it yet," Brazoria County Sheriff's Lt. Matt Wingo said after the remains of two girls were identified ... cal Examiner's office.

The killings first came to light in the mid-1970s when officials found the bodies of a total of 21 girls who had disappeared from three southeast Texas counties in 1971 and 1972.

Wingo said the investigation was rekindled when the bodies of two young girls found five years ago finally were identified as Georgia Geer, 14, and Brooks Bracewell, 12, both of Dickinson.

The girls were both reported missing Dec. 6, 1974.

... other 17 girls reported missing from the same area in 1974 and 1975 may have been killed — bringing the total to 40.

"The girls were mostly 14 or 15 years old," he said. "All came from the same area, had the same or similar hair style and facial appearance. This leads us to believe they were killed by one or two persons, but not more than that."

The bodies of eight of the dead girls identified thus far were found in Brazoria County and the remaining 13 were found in Harris and Galveston ...

Wingo said most of them were shot in the head — "something like an execution-style killing."

He said the remains of the 21 victims were all badly decomposed, but theorized that the victims may have been sexually molested.

"I think it is a sexual thing in that the killer or killers have severe sadistic tendencies," Wingo said. "Most of the bodies were too advanced in decomposition to verify if there had been any sexual molestation.

"The bodies were all dumped on top of the ground and while they weren't actually buried they were ... fully concealed," Wingo said.

Wingo said when the two ... girls' remains were found ... ago, "the investigators at the ... not do a complete search ... found enough just to create a ..."

He said a search last ... same area uncovered ... which helped identify the victi...

He said in light of the latest ... cations, "we plan to go throug... ... reports of the other ki... carefully in hopes of pinning ... actly what it is that links them ..."

San Antonio Express News, April 6, 1981

COLETTE WILSON

Brenda Jones

Gloria Gonzalez

Debbie Ackerman in her last school photo.

Maria Johnson, believed to be her last photo

Bracewell

Geer

Brooks Bracewell and Georgia Geer

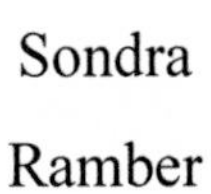

Sondra Ramber

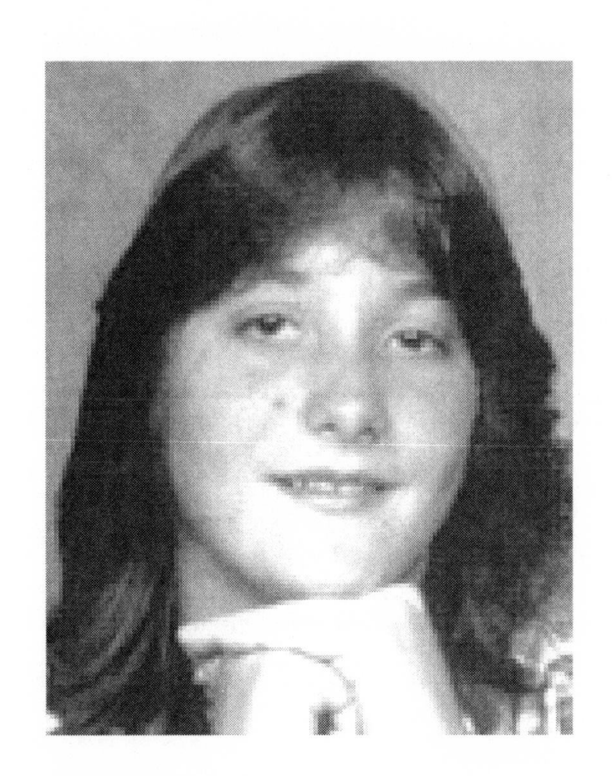

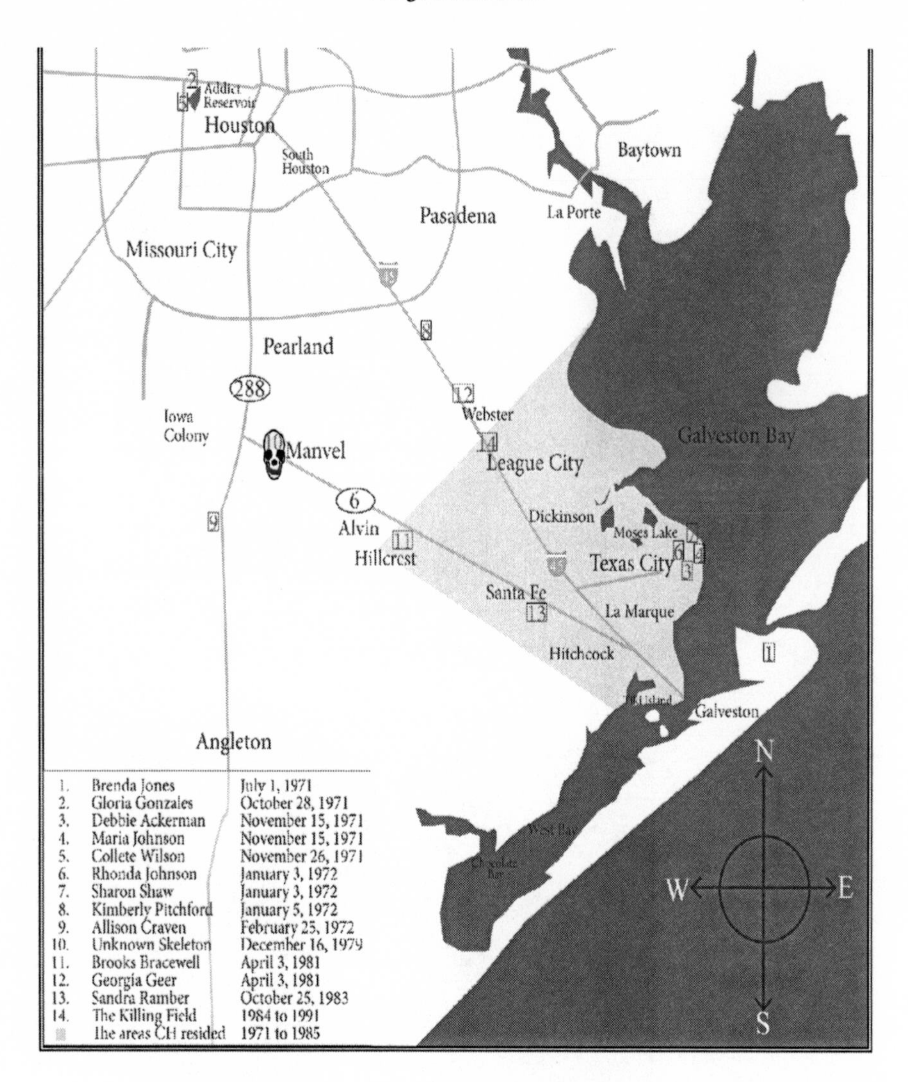

Charlie Hitzfelder Jr. lived at various locations within the highlighted light-gray area from 1971 to 1985.

Covey house in 2009

Hondo Lutheran Church where Carolyn was dropped off on February 14, 1961.

The Hitzfelder Family Home (Circa 2009)

Raye Theater (Circa 2009)

Gate leading to the League City killing fields

Killing field where victims were found near grove of trees

Your Local News Source Since 1842
On the World Wide Web at http://www.galvnews.com
Lee Dougherty, Editor and Publisher Emeritus
Dolph Tillotson, President and Publisher
Heber Taylor, Editor

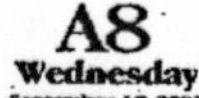
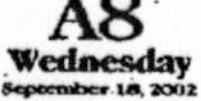

OPINION

A8
Wednesday
September 18, 2002

OUR VIEW

...far until ... break?

BILLIE ... Texas ... will be ...

Molly Ivins

MYSTERIES ALONG I-45

Memory of missing girls will live on

I initially found your special report on the mysteries along the I-45 corridor especially disturbing. A string of kidnappings, assaults, unsolved murders, and disappearances, all within a fairly small radius.

If you add to it the cases of serial killer Donald Leroy Evans, alleged murderer Robert Durst, and the recent Clara Harris drama, it paints a chilling picture of the Galveston area over the past 30 years.

But is it really as bad as it appears on the surface?

Perhaps Galveston isn't simply a magnet for the vilest of psychopaths, but represents a cross section of contemporary society in general.

Please bear with me while I reminisce.

As a kid back in the 1960s, I firmly believed that Galveston was the idyllic community to grow up in.

Lots of warm weather, roaming freely about the town (at least as far as our bare feet could take us on the blistering sidewalks and streets), surfing and fishing along the beach. It was truly an island paradise.

I can still recall, however, the shock and horror that we all felt in 1971 when we learned that two of our Ball High classmates, Maria Johnson and Debbie Ackerman, had been brutally assaulted and coldly murdered.

At that moment our "Huck Finn" existence was forever shattered as our childhood innocence was instantly replaced with the harshness of reality. Two incredibly wonderful girls were taken from our lives forever.

MYSTERIES **Along I-45**

It wasn't too long after Maria and Debbie were killed that my family moved from Galveston and the sadness of that event eventually faded from my memory.

I live in California now, in a small community that, at least for a while, was once as Galveston used to be to a young boy growing up in paradise.

My wife and I have raised two children here and thought that Lancaster was a pretty good place to be. But, times have changed, and I find that our little California town has ignominiously garnered more national attention than it should.

Just a few weeks ago, I was distressed to learn that two of our local high school girls, Tamara Brooks and Jacqueline Marris, had been kidnapped at gunpoint by Roy Ratliff, in nearby Quartz Hill, a neighboring community of Rosamond.

The search was on for their recovery before the unthinkable could happen. Fortunately, both girls were rescued in time and Mr. Ratliff will never again be a threat to society. Afterwards, we all breathed a collective sigh of relief.

I suppose the memory of Maria Johnson and Debbie Ackerman hadn't faded as much as I'd thought.

What saddens me the most, though, about Maria, Debbie and the other 19 cases, is that their story has no ending, happy or otherwise.

My heart goes out to their families and the grief they must live with each day after day, year after year. All we can do is remember the times that they were with us. I know I haven't forgotten them.

Doug Mitchell lives in Lancaster, Calif.

LETTERS TO THE EDITOR

Candidate can't save nomination of judge

I'm not sure I understand what John Cornyn and Texas Republicans thought Ron Kirk could do to save the nomination of Priscilla Owen to the 5th U.S. Circuit Court of Appeals.

He is, after all, only a candidate for the U.S. Senate. If he has this kind of power as a candidate, I am excited to see what wonderful things he'll be able to do after his election!

Elisa Vasquez
Dickinson

Police officer restores faith in Samaritans

On Sept. 9, I was traveling home from Galveston when I had a blowout on the Texas City Wye.

I no sooner got out of my truck to evaluate the situation when Sgt. Gary W. Jones, with Galveston Police Department, pulled over to help me.

He was still in uniform headed home from work. He spent over an hour on the side of the road helping me change my tire. It took him a good while to loosen my spare tire, since it had never been removed since I have owned my truck.

I believe that Sgt. Gary W. Jones acted in a very upstanding way. I am very grateful for his help.

He did not have to help me. I am sure he was ready to get home after a long day at work.

I did not believe there were any Good Samaritans left, but I do now. Thank you.

April Martin
La Marque

DOONESBURY

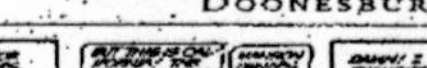

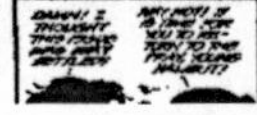

LETTERS POLICY

The Galveston County Daily News welcomes letters of up to 150 words, and gu... to 500 words, on any public issue. Guest columns must include a photograph of... that exceeds the word limit will not be considered for publication. Any guest colu... word limit or does not include a photograph will not be considered for publication... We publish only original letters or guest columns addressed to The Galveston C... An address and daytime phone number must be included so the author's identity...

Galveston Daily News, September 18, 2002

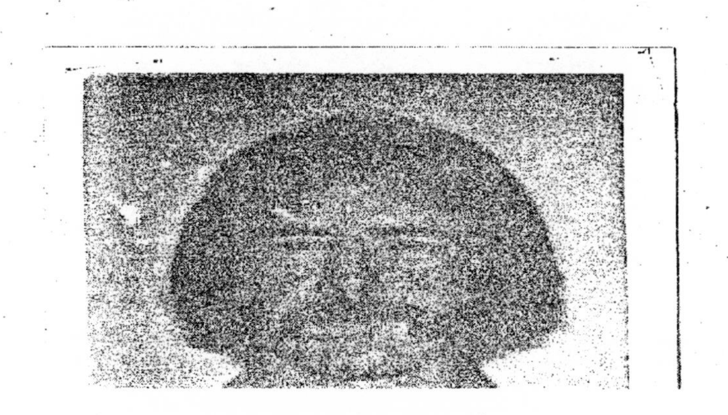

Top photo is a composite of a rape suspect in 1982.

Bottom photo is an early 1980's photo of Charlie Hitzfelder Jr.

Possible site where Claudette was murdered
on February 14, 1961.

TEN
"Til Death Do We Part?"
Charlie's Fourth Marriage: Juanita Hutto-Lamb

In January 1976, Charlie was still working for Can-Go Trucking in Texas City. Charlie's driving record had been cleared of the drunk-driving charge. He was back driving trucks throughout southeast Texas. Charlie moved to Santa Fe, Texas in Galveston County. He often visited a local convenience store, the Mini-Max, where Juanita Hutto-Lamb worked as a cashier. Juanita had two teenage daughters and two teenage sons from a previous marriage. Charlie took an interest in Juanita and visited her almost daily at the store.

Charlie pulled out all the stops and endeared himself to Juanita, acting like a perfect gentleman. Charlie showed great interest in the well being of Juanita's children, impressing her with his concern. He was nice to her and brought her flowers at work. He eventually asked Juanita out on a date. Juanita was struggling to support her children, after just ending her marriage to Jerry Hutto, a severe alcoholic. Juanita told her friends that she still loved Jerry, but she could no longer endure his constant drinking, and mental and physical abuse. She felt she had no choice but to leave Jerry Hutto.

Charlie came into Juanita's life when she was the most vulnerable, being responsible for four teenagers to take care of.

Steven and Beverly, two of Juanita's children, counted on Juanita for support. Juanita was working for minimum wage, telling friends she had nowhere to go. She was desperate. Charlie turned on his charm and acted like a caring man. Charlie began dating Juanita, and in a matter of weeks convinced Juanita he loved her. Charlie promised to care for Juanita and her children. He would be the father they needed. Juanita, Steven and Beverly moved in with Charlie in December 1975. Juanita was desperate for a place to live and needed financial support, so she took a chance. Soon after moving in with Charlie, Juanita agreed to marry him. Charlie and Juanita were married by a justice of the peace in Alvin, Texas on June 6, 1976. Juanita settled into her new life as best she could. A few months later, Charlie moved the family to Santa Fe on SH6, twenty miles northwest of Galveston. Charlie purchased a single-wide mobile home and moved the family into the Lazy Wasp Trailer Park. Steven continued to live with his mother from December 1975 until August 1977 when he married a local girl. Beverly was too young to be on her own and lived with her mother and Charlie. Beverly later told authorities that her so-called happy family did not last very long. Just weeks after the marriage, Charlie's demeanor changed. He got drunk every night and became physically abusive to Juanita and Beverly. Juanita soon realized she made a mistake marrying Charlie. She wanted out of the marriage, but did not know what to do, as she had no place to go.

Over the next few years, life was very hard in the Hitzfelder trailer. Charlie's physical abuse of Juanita increased as the days dragged on. On occasion, Juanita would get fed up with the abuse and leave Charlie for a day or two. Beverly told others she did not understand why her mother stayed with such a terrible man. Beverly recounted that her father, Jerry, was also abusive. At her young age, she accepted that men were like that.

January 13, 1980 was a very tragic day for the Hutto children. Beverly was home alone when she received a telephone call from Charlie Jr. He said her mother was in Galveston County Hospital and very sick due to a heart attack. Beverly said that when she heard this news, she questioned how her mother could have a heart attack. Beverly's mother was forty-two and in good health. Beverly called her brother, Stephen, and broke the news. Steven drove to the trailer, picked up his sister and drove to the hospital. When they arrived, Steven and Beverly learned that their mother was in the intensive care unit. Hospital staff said they thought Juanita suffered a heart attack. They reported that Juanita had made it through the rough part and that she should be fine. Juanita was in a room recovering. Beverly and Steven were shocked, as Juanita had no history of heart problems. One of the nurses said that Charlie Jr. was at Juanita's side.

Beverly asked the nurse how her mother could have had a heart attack, as she was not obese and did not have medical problems common to people who suffer from heart disease.

The nurse could not answer Beverly's question. Steven and Beverly went to the room where Juanita was recovering. Charlie met both children at the door and told them that their mother was very ill. He said they could not go inside the room to see her because of doctor's orders. Beverly was worried and wanted to comfort her mother. She walked to a nearby nursing station and asked why she and he brother could not see their mother. They were told that Charlie was her husband and if did not want anyone to see her, there was nothing they could do. The nurses did not want to upset Juanita who was still very sick. Beverly was told they could see their mother the next morning. She was not happy, but took the nurse's advice and waited until the next morning to see her mother. While Beverly was at the nurse's station, Charlie let Steven see his mother, but only for a minute or two. Steven went into the room and asked his mother to open her eyes. Juanita opened her eyes and grabbed his hand. She asked Steven what was wrong with her. Charlie told Steven that his mother wanted to be left alone and was told to come back later.

The next morning, Beverly and Steven returned to the hospital to see Juanita. When they arrived at the hospital, they were told that their mother had another heart attack and died. They were devastated. Charlie was still at the hospital. Charlie appeared very upset and concerned over the specific cause of death. Both children thought this was odd he was so concerned but there was nothing they could do.

Charlie decided to have Juanita buried at the Grace Memorial Cemetery in Hitchcock. He arranged a nice service and ordered a dual-headstone. The family name Hitzfelder was boldly displayed.

Juanita's name was also carved on the headstone, along with the dates 1937 to 1980. Charlie also had the stone carved with the words: Charles J. Jr., 1942 to _____. This inscription was carved to the left of Juanita's name. Charlie played the perfect grieving widower. He told all who would listen to him that Juanita was the love of his life. He could never be happy with anyone else again. After Juanita's death, Beverly did not go back to live with Charlie. She stayed with Steven and his wife, as well as other friends. She was deathly afraid of Charlie. Steven did not believe his sister when she told him that Charlie often beat their mother. Steven seemed appreciative that Charlie bought them food and clothes. He felt Charlie did more for him than his own father.

About eight months after their mother's death, Steven and Beverly gave their accounts of life with Charlie Hitzfelder. There was a stark contrast between Steven and Beverly's feelings as to what kind of a man Charlie was. Steven did not remember his mother having arguments or fights with Charlie. He said he never knew anything about his mother's repeated beatings. He felt his mother would have confided in him, as he was close to her. In contrast, he said his mother bossed Charlie around. He was aware that Charlie had a temper, but he said he never saw Charlie hit her. He felt that Charlie was a good provider, remembering the food and clothing he bought them. As far as Steven was concerned, Charlie was a pretty good guy. This was in spite of Charlie being accused of killing a girl in Hondo. Charlie told Steven that a girl was killed when Charlie was eighteen. Charlie said the police came and took him back to Hondo, but found the killer and he was cleared.

Immediately after her death, Steven asked Charlie how his mother died. Charlie told him that his mother died from a stage five heart valve blockage. This sounded like a reasonable explanation and he was satisfied with the cause of death. At the time, he was sure that the police would have told him if they suspected foul play in his mother's death. Steven told the police that when Charlie had a few beers, his attitude and personality would change, making him a little weird. Charlie kept the door to his bedroom locked at all times, keeping others out of his room. He was strange about that room for some reason.

Beverly Hutto told others that Charlie was "a mean son-of-a-bitch," and beat her mother often. Charlie would hit Juanita with his fists, slap her, and even kick her in the stomach. One day at the trailer Charlie was drunk and she watched him kick Juanita and slap her in the face. Juanita ran out the door and Charlie chased after her. He caught up to her and used both arms to drag her back into the house by her hair. She saw Charlie kicking Juanita in the stomach and back several more times with his boots. Because of the beating, Juanita had several knots on her head and bruises all over her body.

On other occasions, Charlie slapped Juanita around, beating her so badly she could not take it anymore. During one of those arguments, Juanita opened a kitchen drawer and pulled out a knife to defend her self. This made Charlie laugh like a crazy man. He grabbed the knife and swung it at Juanita over and over, just missing her head as he laughed. Between the laughter, Charlie said, "How do you like this, bitch? It hurts, doesn't it?" Finally, Juanita sat down on the couch and lit a cigarette. Charlie walked over to Juanita as she sat on the couch, still holding the knife, swinging it and cutting the cigarette off at the filter.

Beverly recalled a night when Charlie almost killed Juanita. The two were arguing about Charlie's drinking. Charlie went out to his car and came back into the house with a big smile on his face. Charlie was holding a pistol in his hand. He put the gun to Juanita's head and said, "Life is short, and it can end with a bullet or maybe two to your head." He said he was going to kill Juanita and then himself. When Charlie was drunk, he often beat holes in the walls and doors of the trailer with his fists. When angry at Juanita, he would hit her or take it out on the trailer.

Charlie was a strange man, never allowing Juanita's friends to visit the house. He virtually kept her a prisoner at times. Juanita had a friend named Sara, who Charlie hated. In spite of that, Sara would visit anyway. If Charlie was home when Sara left, he would beat Juanita, telling her he did not want Sara around his house.

Whenever Charlie drank alcohol, he got mean and nasty, going into rages and throwing fits, but could still walk a straight line and drive his car. Charlie's hangovers were so severe he would throw up in the toilet. Charlie would complain that he could not remember what happened the night before. When Charlie was sober, his attitude was better, but he still was mean. Charlie would often tell Juanita that he was sorry for what he did the night before.

Charlie thought he was better than other people, often putting people down. He did not have a nice thing to say about anyone. Charlie would start arguments when someone he did not like was mentioned in his house. Charlie's comments about these people were awful. If he was talking about a woman, he would call her a bitch. If he was talking about a man, he would call him an asshole. Charlie had no friends. No one liked Charlie, and it was easy to see why. Charlie did not like anyone but himself. Charlie used drugs, taking black mollies when driving his work truck. Charlie took the pills to stay awake, but several times took those same pills when not working. He would take the pills and then drink beer. He also smoked marijuana, while making offensive comments about others who smoked marijuana. Charlie would call them potheads or drug addicts. Sometimes when Charlie got drunk, he would act like a baby, sitting on the couch and whining about things. Juanita would often help Charlie to bed.

Before her marriage, Juanita received a telephone call from a woman named Melanie, who said she was Charlie's ex-wife. Melanie called to warn her not to marry Charlie. Juanita learned that Charlie would beat Melanie on a regularly basis. In spite of these warnings, Juanita married Charlie.

One Christmas, Charlie took Juanita and Beverly to Hondo to visit his mother and father. Charlie's father told them that when he was the sheriff he once killed a bunch of Mexicans. He said that as sheriff he shot more than one wetback Mexican between the eyes. Charlie Sr. continued to brag, stating "he hated Mexicans and enjoyed shooting them".

While on a drive with his family, Charlie told them he dated a girl in Hondo who ended up getting killed. Charlie said he was innocent of her murder. He claimed that someone running for sheriff had tried to frame him for the murder.

Charlie said the man running against his father was trying to smear the family name. According to Charlie Jr., they finally arrested a mental patient for the girl's murder, clearing Charlie of any involvement.

When Juanita first married Charlie, Beverly's girlfriends often visited. Charlie would come outside and watch them play, finding a way to get involved in what they were doing. Charlie would play-wrestle with the girls, grabbing them from behind and lifting them off the ground. As he lifted them up, he would place his hands on their breasts. Beverly now believes he was trying to molest the girls. She saw him try to pull the shorts down on a few of her girlfriends. One girl, who lived next door, came to the house when Charlie was at work. The girl told Beverly she was not coming over to the house anymore. She confided that Charlie scared her to death. He played too rough, pinching her breasts and feeling around her vagina. Beverly wondered why her mother did nothing when she learned this. Other girlfriends told Beverly that Charlie did the same kind of things to them. One of her friends from school said Charlie grabbed her bra and pulled it off, exposing her breasts. When Charlie pulled her bra off, he laughed. She yelled at him, and he grabbed her arm and told her she didn't want him mad at her.

Before Juanita died, she confided to Beverly that Charlie tried on several occasions to molest her little sister, Sandra. Juanita walked in on Charlie and Sandra, catching him in the act. Charlie explained that he was only playing with Sandra. Juanita must have believed something was wrong, because Sandra moved away to stay with other family members. Beverly could not explain why Juanita stayed with Charlie after this incident.

One day, when the family was living in Santa Fe, Charlie yelled at Sandra for no particular reason. Sandra talked back to Charlie, yelling at him to leave her alone. In response, Charlie kicked Sandra in the butt. Sandra's boyfriend was in the trailer at the time. He got very angry with Charlie for doing this. Sandra's boyfriend was only seventeen, but got up and chased Charlie out the door. Sandra's boyfriend told Charlie that men who hit on girls were little cowards. After Juanita died, Charlie began acting even stranger. He would not let anyone in their bedroom. Charlie complained that there were spirits in the room For some reason; Charlie was worried about how his dad would react to Juanita's death. He began acting so weirdly; Beverly stayed away from the house as much as she could.

Before Juanita died, she confided to Beverly that she feared she was going to die. She did not say why she felt this way. She told Beverly to take back whatever she bought for her after her death. During the months leading up to her death, Beverly said Juanita would have bad fights with Charlie. Juanita was so afraid of Charlie she did not want to be left alone with him, ever.

One day, Juanita hid Charlie's gun. She was afraid Charlie was going to kill her. On another occasion, Charlie got mad at Juanita and went into the kitchen and got a bucket of ice water. Charlie went into Juanita's room and poured the water all over her underpants. Charlie had some kind of fetish about women's panties. He insisted on buying all Juanita's underpants. Shortly after they married, Charlie took a knife and cut up all Juanita's underpants. Charlie told Juanita that he would take her shopping and pick out the types he liked. After Juanita died, Charlie said he could no longer dream, waking up in the middle of the night crying. He complained of bad headaches. The entire time the family lived with Charlie, he could not sleep at night and complained of severe headaches when he drank. The family could not understand why he drank if it caused him to get sick.

When the family lived with Charlie, he drove a white 1957 Chevrolet pickup. He treated the truck like it was his baby, his pride and joy. Charlie also told them that his father was mad at him for a bad loan he helped arrange. Charlie said that throughout his life, his father said he never wanted a son. This seemed to way heavily on Charlie, insisting his parents treated him badly when he was growing up. Charlie stayed with his grandparents as often as he could. He said his grandparents practically raised him. In December 1977, Juanita tried to leave Charlie and move back with her ex-husband Jerry. Juanita really loved Jerry, but he too was an alcoholic. Jerry could not support her, so she moved back in with Charlie.

Charlie only talked about one friend, C.W. Ellis, who lived in nearby Algoa. Charlie mentioned his name a few times. When Charlie and Juanita were together, they did not have any close friends. Charlie did not like having friends, telling Juanita that they were best friends and did not need anyone else.

Charlie's Fifth Marriage: Patricia Ellis-Sweet "Monster of a Man"

In April 1980, Charlie Hitzfelder Jr. continued to work for Can-Go Trucking as a dispatcher and part time driver. On occasion he would drive truck routes. At this time a single-mother, Patricia Ellis-Sweet, worked in the same office. Patricia was thirty-seven and an attractive woman, tall and slender. She was 5'10" tall, weighed 145 pounds, and had light red hair. Patricia was raising three small children: Frances was twelve, Eva was eleven, and Wesley was nine. The children attended middle-school, while living in Dickenson, Texas on Patricia's parents' property. Patricia was a very accommodating but quiet woman, who had recently divorced Wesley Sweet. Her marriage to Wesley was fraught with his infidelity. She found it hard to complain about slights and even harder to leave him. When she finally did complain, it was after she was on her own.

Charlie owned a single-wide mobile home he had purchased in 1977. Charlie was single again because Juanita had died suddenly and unexpectedly of a heart attack a few months earlier on January 14, 1980. One afternoon while at work, Charlie asked Patricia out for a date. At first, Patricia was somewhat reluctant, feeling nervous about Charlie, afraid she might be making a big mistake. For some reason, she decided to go out with Charlie. On their first date, Charlie took Patricia to the Las Cocina dance club. It was not far from Can-Go Trucking. Patricia was impressed that Charlie did not drink alcohol, even though it was served at the club. Patricia and Charlie talked and drank coffee for an hour or so. She told her children that Charlie seemed to be a kind man. On that first date, Charlie and Patricia danced to country western songs for several hours. Charlie was a complete gentleman. To Patricia, the date was a success. Over the next three to four months, Charlie and Patricia continued to date on weekends and occasionally after work. During this time, Charlie treated Patricia well. However, there was one warning sign about Charlie's personality that Patricia unwittingly overlooked. Charlie began drinking beer and whiskey on their dates. Although he was often drunk by the end of the night, he still seemed attentive to Patricia's children. For the most part, Charlie seemed like a nice person.

On April Fools Day in 1980, Charlie surprised Patricia during dinner, asking her to marry him. Patricia thought about her other bad previous relationships. With all her heart, she hoped this relationship and marriage would be the one she had always hoped for. Patricia agreed to marry Charlie.

On July 2, 1980, Charlie, Patricia, and her children drove to Port Arthur, Texas, where they were married by a justice of the peace. Patricia's sister, Brenda McFadden, also attended the ceremony. After the ceremony, the family went out for dinner and spent the night at a local motel. The next day, they all headed back to Dickenson.

Soon after the wedding, Patricia and the children moved into Charlie's trailer at the Lazy Wasp Trailer Park. A few months later, Charlie moved the trailer onto a parcel of land owned by Patricia's family. The small parcel of land was located in an unincorporated portion of Dickenson, Texas.

Charlie's daily demeanor soon changed, beginning his days with whiskey and beer, and ending them drunk. As before, when Charlie drank, he became loud, profane, and rude, threatening Patricia and the children. Charlie's verbal assaults on the family soon led to physical abuse. He would slap Patricia in the face without provocation, or shove her around the trailer for any perceived slight. Patricia had recently left a brutal relationship, leading her to believe Charlie's behavior and treatment of her was normal. Although fearful of Charlie, she did nothing to stop his cruelty. Charlie would often complain of headaches after a drinking binge and without provocation ramp up his physically beatings of Patricia. Charlie would often come home from work in a terrible mood. He often yelled at Patricia's children and got upset if there was no milk in the refrigerator. He demanded the Sweet children call him daddy.

Frances, Patricia's oldest daughter said Charlie often screamed at them in a loud, threatening tone, demanding to know who drank the last bit of milk or if they had cleaned the kitchen. Frances was deathly afraid of Charlie, as were her brother and sister. Frances learned early on that even if she had not done anything wrong, it was best to reply that she had. She knew that upsetting Charlie came with a cost. Charlie was emotionally volatile, so Frances did not want to challenge his authority, fearing a beating. Frances said Charlie seemed to have two personalities, switching from one to the other without notice. He would not let her friend's visit, which was okay with the Frances, as her friends were also terrified by what Charlie might do or say.

When Frances was twelve, she was 5'4" tall, with shoulder-length brown hair and brown eyes. She had a medium complexion and people told her she was pretty. For a two-year period Charlie sexually mistreated her. His abuse may have included sexual intercourse. Frances revealed that her birth father molested her from an early age, and she continues to repress the memories of bad things in her life. Within a few weeks of the marriage, Charlie demanded that Frances massage his back, taking her into his bedroom and having her to sit on his back. Eventually he ordered Frances to massage his chest, stomach, and legs. This even happened when Patricia was home.

During these massages, Charlie asked Frances if she thought there was an afterlife, if there was a heaven. Frances would say that she believed in heaven. Charlie would respond that there was no heaven, only a hell. He would also frighten Frances saying, "Little girls like you can end up dead if you are not careful. It happens all the time." For twenty-five years Frances did not reveal that Charlie had touched her inappropriately. She wasn't sure, or perhaps couldn't remember, but she believed Charlie might have forced her to have intercourse with him. This was such a terrible time in her life; she never wanted to talk about these events. She was afraid to tell her mother Charlie had been molesting her.

Patricia would have blamed herself. Patricia tried to take good care of her children, while she was a battered woman.

Charlie often used illegal drugs like black mollies, roofies, and yellow jackets. These pills helped Charlie Junior stay up for long periods of time while driving over-the-road. He often told Frances to go out to his green Ford to retrieve a bag of pills. Charlie would spill the pills onto a table and count them. Frances was not sure, but suspects Charlie may have secretly given her some of the drugs. She recalled often falling to sleep for no apparent reason. This usually happened when she was alone with Charlie, waking up in Charlie's bed without her clothes on. Charlie also took her out alone for drives at night, cruising country roads for hours. She asked Charlie what they were doing, and he responded, "Looking around."

Charlie's physical abuse was not limited to Patricia and Frances. Charlie occasionally kicked Frances' nine-year-old brother, Wesley, for no reason whatsoever. From time to time, Charlie would get out his pistol and point the gun at Patricia and the children, cautioning them not to make him mad. The children lived in fear of what Charlie might do next.

Patricia was helpless, exhibiting the signs of a woman too afraid to leave an abusive man, who engaged in sexual and physical violence. As with prior marriages, Charlie did weird things like cutting up all of Patricia's underpants. Frances remains deathly afraid of Charlie.

When Patricia was first interviewed for this book, she was not aware that Charlie had died. Patricia would not speak about Charlie until local police authorities confirmed he was dead. She remained terrified of Charlie decades later. Patricia told a tragic tale of horrific sexual, physical, and mental abuse throughout her marriage. Charlie often forced her to perform oral sex on him, while holding a loaded gun to her head. At these moments, Charlie would say, "How would you like to have some bullet holes in your skull? You had best do what I say." Charlie had forced Patricia to perform oral sex in front of her children, demeaning, embarrassing, and humiliating Patricia and her children. He would also walk up behind her, grabbing her by the throat, choking her with one hand while wielding a knife in the other. On New Year's Eve 1981, Patricia and Charlie attended a party at one of Patricia's friend's homes. Her children were spending time with their birth father, Wesley, that week. When they arrived at the party, Patricia saw that there were not enough chairs. As a joke, two of her male friends locked their arms and hands together, making a seat for her. Patricia thought this was funny, so she sat down on their arms laughing. Charlie got very angry. He stormed out of the party and drove off. To her surprise, Charlie returned to the party twenty minutes later. He walked up to Patricia who was sitting on a couch in the front room, talking with some of her girlfriends. Charlie lifted his coat, putting his hand on a gun tucked into his waistband. He told her to come with him or he would kill her. Terrified and fearing for her life, she did not say a word. Patricia got up and walked out with Charlie. Her friends were stunned but did not say a word to Patricia or Charlie. She got into the car with Charlie and on the ride home; he repeatedly punched her in the face, telling her over and over that he was going to kill her for what she done to him. He kept asking her why she was messing with those men. She was too afraid to answer him and kept silent on the way home. When they arrived at the trailer, Patricia had already endured quite a beating. Charlie yelled at to her to get inside in the trailer. She did what she was told. As she walked, Charlie followed close behind. Charlie hit her in the back of her head with a half-full whiskey bottle as she walked up the steps. The glass broke, opening a severe gash. Bleeding and soaked with whiskey, she went inside the trailer. Charlie continued to slap her and hit her with his fists. He would not allow Patricia to get medical attention, telling her to put a rag on her head to stop the bleeding. Charlie grabbed his gun, took his clothes off, and asked Patricia, "Do you want to mess with me? Do you want to die tonight?" Charlie walked over to Patricia and told her to get down on her knees. Charlie put the gun to the back of Patricia's head and told her she was a no good bitch. He told her to put his penis in her mouth, as he held his penis in one hand and the gun in the other.

She did what he said, as he asked over and over if she wanted to die. Patricia did what he asked, but he was unable to have an organism. This often happened to him. Patricia suspected Charlie liked having oral sex to frighten her to death, rather than to achieve orgasm. After awhile, Charlie's intoxication made him shaky on his feet. He went to his bedroom and passed out on the bed. The bleeding from Patricia's head wound slowed down after twenty minutes.

When Patricia thought it was safe, she sneaked out of the house and drove to David Bradley's house. David was once her brother-in-law. She pleaded with him to let her stay at his house. David agreed, hiding her car from Charlie. David told Patricia over and over to call the police. Patricia always refused to call the police and report Charlie's abuse. She feared that when he got out of jail, he would kill her and the children. Patricia telephoned her ex-husband, Wesley, asking him not to return the kids to the trailer. She did not tell him Charlie had beaten her. She knew Wesley might kill or be killed by Charlie. She told Wesley they had an argument. The next morning, Patricia went to a nearby clinic and had her head injury stitched up. She lied to the doctor, telling him she had fallen down.

A day later, Charlie tracked Patricia down at David Bradley's house. He asked David if he could speak to her. David asked Charlie if he was going to be violent. Charlie looked surprised and said he had never hit a woman. Charlie told David that he would be a complete gentleman. Charlie told Patricia he was sorry about how he had acted and promised to never behave that way again. Patricia was so battered and accommodating; she agreed to go back to Charlie. David could not believe this, and told Patricia he would not help her out again. There was little David could do to stop her. Today, she wishes she had listened to David.

Over the next year, Charlie, of course, broke his word. His violent outrages continued. One afternoon, following a fight, Patricia went her mother's house. Charlie followed and asked Patricia's mother if he could speak to her. Patricia's mother, also named Frances, told Charlie that he'd best not harm her daughter. Charlie told Frances that he would change his ways and treat Patricia like a princess. Patricia's mother never liked Charlie, always suspicious of his motives. She agreed to let Charlie speak to Patricia, but kept a close eye on them as they talked. Charlie and Patricia went into the yard and sat on a swing. Charlie begged Patricia to come back to him, telling her he loved her, promising to never hurt her again.

Charlie literally begged her to come home. Patricia said she was scared for her children. Charlie promised to be nice to them. Patricia was apprehensive and told Charlie she wanted to think about coming back to him. She walked into the house. Charlie was furious that she had not given into him. He followed her into the house as she walked to the kitchen sink. Charlie came up behind her and began choking her. Patricia's mother jumped up from the couch and ran into the kitchen with a large knife in her hand. She threatened to cut off both Charlie's hands and arms if he didn't leave her alone. Charlie loosened his grasp on Patricia's throat and turned toward her mother. He began to cry like a baby. He was trembling all over. Patricia stood there stunned. After several minutes, Charlie was composed enough to leave the house. After Charlie left, Patricia's mother told her to call the police, but she refused. Her mother warned that Charlie was going to kill her. She would not listen. Later that night, against the wishes of her mother and family members, Patricia returned home to Charlie.

Another brutal incident occurred one evening when Patricia and the children were visiting family friends, the Benitas. Patricia and her kids were not home by Charlie's dinnertime. Charlie got his pistol and drove around Dickenson looking for Patricia's car. He parked his car and stormed into the Benitas' house without knocking. He called Patricia a slut and asked where she had been. He asked Patricia what was wrong with her and threatened to kill all of them if they didn't listen to him. Charlie hit Wesley on his back with the butt of his gun, knocking him to the floor. Charlie then pushed Frances over the front room table. Eva was so afraid she ran out of the house and got into Charlie's car. Patricia yelled at her children to go. Mrs. Benita was terrified by the brutality and considered calling the police, but remembered Patricia telling her that Charlie would kill her and the kids if the police were ever called.

One day, Charlie found Patricia and Wesley at a nearby minimart. He was furious that Patricia was not at home when he returned from work. He had driven around on his Gold Wing Honda until he found Patricia leaving the store. She tried to drive off, but Charlie chased her, swinging a long chain at the car. When the chain hooked the car's bumper, Charlie dumped his motorcycle in the parking lot. Charlie suffered minor cuts and abrasions. Patricia drove off, leaving Charlie in the parking lot.

The family was constantly in fear for their safety, but Patricia was more afraid to leave Charlie. The children wanted to please their mother and realized what a desperate situation it was for her. They knew Patricia did not have the strength or fortitude to leave. The children tried hard to please Charlie, for their mother's benefit.

In January 1982, Charlie met another woman. Debra Jo Biggs lived in the Bay Cliff area of Galveston. She was a single mother with pre-teen children. Charlie began dating Debbie while still married to Patricia. He did not hide his latest infatuation, telling Patricia and the children he found another woman. He bragged that Debbie's children wanted him to be their dad. Patricia and the kids were stunned at his news, but also very happy Charlie had a new love. Charlie told Patricia that he wanted a divorce. Patricia would soon be free of this monster of a man.

Over the next few weeks, Charlie filed court papers in Galveston County. The uncontested divorce was official on July 19, 1982. While waiting for the divorce to be final, Charlie was rarely home. He spent his free time with Debbie and her children in Bay Cliff to the delight of Patricia and her children. A few days before the divorce was final, Patricia and the kids moved back to her parents' home. Charlie kept his mobile home.

In late June 1982, Charlie took Debbie to Can Go Trucking on his motorcycle to pick up his paycheck. Patricia was working in the office, where she was well liked by the office manager. When Charlie rode up with his new girlfriend, the office manager was outraged. He could not believe Charlie could be so cold-blooded as to bring his new girlfriend to work just to embarrass Patricia. The manager called Charlie aside and told him he could not believe he was such a bastard. He fired Charlie on the spot. Charlie appeared devastated, but said nothing. He took his check, walked outside, jumped on his motorcycle, and peeled out of the parking lot. Before the divorce was final, Patricia agreed to let Charlie stay on the family land with his trailer for one year. She did not want to create anymore problems with Charlie.

On July 21, 1982, two days after the divorce to Patricia was final, Charlie and Deborah Biggs were married in a civil ceremony performed by a justice of the peace in Brazoria County. Six months later, Charlie called Patricia to tell her his trailer was going to be repossessed by the bank. He was broke and could not make the payments.

A day or so after this phone call, Charlie showed up at Patricia's new employer, Bay Area Disposal. Charlie brought a small portable television with him. He said he wanted to give the television back to her and that he felt bad about the way he treated her. Patricia noticed that Charlie's face was bruised, as if he had been in a fight. She asked what happened to him. Charlie told her that Debbie's brothers beat him up. The brothers told Charlie they were going to kill him. Patricia learned that Debbie, the kids, and Charlie were moving to his grandparents' home in Medina County. Charlie asked to borrow money from Patricia. She told him she only had $20. Charlie told her that would have to do. Patricia took the television and Charlie took the money. Charlie drove off on his motorcycle and was never seen again by Patricia and her children.

Some moths after Charlie moved to Medina County, Patricia received a telephone call from Debbie Biggs, now Debbie Hitzfelder. She told Patricia that she was so lucky she had gotten away from Charlie. She said she left Charlie and moved back to Bay Cliff after several beatings. He knocked out Debbie's front teeth. Debbie told Patricia that she hoped Charlie did not follow her because she believed her brothers would kill him.

Frances Sweet had two possible connections between Charlie Hitzfelder Jr. and the missing and murdered girls found along the I-45 corridor between Galveston and Houston. Frances' sister Eva had a girlfriend named Sondra Ramber in 1982. Sondra was fourteen and from Santa Fe. Sondra Ramber disappeared on October 23, 1983.

Frances' sister, Eva, attended school with Sondra. At the time of Sondra's disappearance, Frances' mother, Patricia, was dating Sondra Ramber's father, Alton Ramber. Police never investigated this connection. The disappearance and presumed murder of Sondra Ramber remains unsolved. Frances said Charlie would often come to the skating rink in Dickenson where Sondra, Eva and Frances would skate. Frances is certain that Charlie knew Sondra from activities such as skating, volleyball and other school activities.

Another possible connection between Charlie and the missing and dead girls in the Galveston area came in the late 1990s. Jonathan Drew was arrested in Webster, Texas after being stopped by the police. Tina Flood, who had been beaten so badly, she was barely alive, was in Drew's car. She later died. Drew was arrested and convicted of Tina's murder.

A few years before, Jonathan raped thirteen-year-old Wendy Ruffini. Wendy lived in Seabrook, Texas. Wendy's rape was not initially reported. At Jonathan Drew's murder trial, the rape was disclosed. The connection to Charlie Hitzfelder was simple: Wendy and Frances were close friends in 1982. Later in life, Wendy was related to Frances by marriage. In Frances' mind, Charlie had to know Wendy. Drew once lived on Humble Camp Road, where the bodies of Debbie Ackerman and Maria Johnson were found in 1971. Charlie Hitzfelder also lived on Humble Camp Road on the Sweet property. It is very possible that Drew and Charlie knew one another. There is no record that any law enforcement official looked into this connection.

In 1981, Eddie Barr of the Galveston County Sheriff's Department said the Ackerman and Johnson girls were last seen about eight blocks from where Charlie was living at the time. Further, the girls' bodies were found was less than two miles from Can-Go Trucking, where Charlie worked at the time.

Finally, Eddie Barr's investigation in 1980 and 1982 determined that while Charlie worked for Can-Co Trucking he had access to the keys of abandoned oil field slush pits, similar to the one where the remains of Debbie Ackerman and Maria Johnson were found. Charlie often visited these sites to pump slush from the fields. Eddie remembered following Charlie one day to a remote part of Humble Camp Road. Charlie stopped his car at the gate leading to the area where the girls were found in the Turner Bayou. He sat in his car for about ten minutes. Eddie's investigation revealed that Charlie was staying on Sweet family land at the time. There was no reason for Charlie to stop and stare into the field. As law enforcement officers, we know that offenders often revisit the site of a murder.

Santa Fe Police detectives believed that Charlie also had keys to the Cader Road killing fields in League City. At the Cader Road site, four young girls' bodies were later found. The method of death for two of the girls bore a striking resemblance to the 1961 murder of Carolyn Covey, as well as other murdered girls. It is plausible that Charlie was a friend of Jonathan Drew. As police investigators, we know that the likelihood of two serial killers living so close to one another, and not be associated, is very remote. Both men were apparently also acquainted with Wendy Ruffini, who Jonathan Drew was accused of raping.

Charlie's Sixth Marriage: Deborah Biggs "He Was a Mean Son-of-a-Bitch"

Today, Debbie Biggs lives in a small travel trailer in her mother's backyard. She works at an animal shelter and still anguishes over her marriage to Charlie Hitzfelder. When she married Charlie Jr., Debbie was 5'7" tall and weighed ninety-nine pounds. Her dark complexion made her look Hispanic. She had reddish-brown hair and brown eyes, looking very similar to Claudette Carolyn Covey, only older.

In 1979, Debbie was a single mother with two small children. She had a ten-year-old son and a six-year-old daughter. Debbie worked at her parents' gasoline station, Don's Texaco, located on Telephone Road and Loop 610 in the southern portion of Houston. Debbie was a cashier. One day, she met a delivery man named Charlie Hitzfelder, who worked for U-need-A. The company exchanged dirty uniforms and rags for clean ones, supplying gasoline stations and auto mechanics. Charlie exchanged clean rags and uniforms for dirty ones weekly. Charlie was very polite and flirty with Debbie at first. He was a gentleman, opening doors for her and smiling all the time. She was aware that Charlie was married to Juanita Lamb. In spite of that, they began a friendship. At first, Charlie would take her to lunch. Later, as time progressed he would take her out on dinner dates. Soon their relationship became sexual. Generally, they only went out once or twice per month. Charlie came into the station one day and told Debbie that his wife, Juanita had suffered a heart attack and died. Debbie believed Charlie was devastated over Juanita's death.

Although Charlie said he was still grieving over his loss, it was only one week until he asked Debbie out on a date again. He said that he wanted to spend more time with her. Their time together increased until a few months later. Out of the blue, Charlie told Debbie he was going to marry a woman named Patricia, who had a couple of young children. Debbie finally realized that Charlie had been seeing other women when they were dating. At the time, Debbie was not interested in marrying Charlie—so she overlooked his other women. After Charlie married Patricia, he often visited Debbie on his route, taking Debbie out to lunch and dinner. Although Charlie was recently married, he and Debbie continued to be involved sexually. Debbie said that Charlie's sexual habits and traits were normal as far as she was concerned, although she was reluctant to speak about this subject. By now Charlie had been with two other women while he had been dating Debbie. But she continued seeing Charlie after he married because he kept telling Debbie he had made a mistake in marrying Patricia.

Charlie was very polite when they first met, but he soon turned into a different man. Finally one day, Charlie told Debbie that he loved her and wanted to get out of his marriage with Patricia. Prior to meeting Charlie, the men in Debbie's life often beat her and treated her badly. Debbie believed this was the way men treated women. Because of this, she did not question it when Charlie started beating her. Almost from the beginning, Charlie would be physical to her—first by slapping her on the face for little provocation. Charlie escalated his abuse breaking her nose on day.

Because of Debbie's history with domestic abuse, she did not understand what a normal relationship entailed. When Charlie drank, he would beat Debbie. When he sobered up, he would apologize. Like Charlie's other victims, Debbie endured his beatings out of her fear and familiarity with this type of treatment. Over time, she began to fear for her life. Charlie threatened to kill her if she told anyone about the beatings. Debbie believed him. She was also concerned about what Charlie might do to her children. In retrospect, she believes she was naive for not leaving Charlie sooner than she did.

One afternoon, Charlie had the day off. He and Debbie drove to Santa Fe to visit Grace Memorial Cemetery. Charlie said he wanted to check on Juanita's grave. When they got to her grave, Charlie got on his knees and placed his hands on Juanita's headstone. He started talking to Juanita, as if she could actually hear him. This behavior was so bizarre it frightened Debbie, who suspected Charlie must be crazy. After a few minutes, Charlie turned to Debbie and told her that he had personally had something to do with Juanita's death. Charlie said that on the day Juanita died, the two were arguing about money and other things. Charlie said he lost his temper and beat Juanita badly. He kicked her in the stomach over and over. About an hour after the beating, she started complaining of chest pains. Charlie ignored her complaints for several hours, but finally began to worry that she might die. He decided to take her to the hospital in Galveston. Charlie said that as they drove to the hospital, he warned Juanita not to mention his beating her. Charlie told Juanita she would end up dead if she said anything about his abuse of her. He added that he would also kill her children. Charlie told Debbie that immediately after Juanita's death he was afraid he would be arrested for killing her. Charlie was surprised the police never questioned him. Debbie said that all this talk made her secure in believing that if she crossed Charlie, she could end up like Juanita.

Charlie's constant drinking became worse. Each time he got drunk, his personality would dramatically change. He became violent and brutal to Debbie, as well as anyone else who was around. Debbie never knew what type of behavior would come next when Charlie drank Jack Daniel's and beer. It was amazing how much Charlie could drink. But once intoxicated, his demeanor would change from somewhat likeable, to loud and profane. Debbie remembers the details of a few of her beatings, even to this day. On one occasion they were going to have dinner at Gallagher's Restaurant in Houston. Charlie accidentally locked his keys in the car, making him angry, so he punched out one of the truck's windows. At the time he was driving a yellow Chevrolet Luv pickup truck, trimmed in orange. They did not go inside to eat; Charlie just drove off. After Charlie calmed down, they stopped at a Church's Chicken. He went inside and bought dinner to go. As they were driving home, Charlie got angry with Debbie for no apparent reason. When they got home, he beat her, kicking her in the stomach and throwing beer and coleslaw over her head. He nearly sent her to the hospital.

Another incident happened when Charlie and Debbie were at her mother's home in San Leon. Charlie got extremely drunk, following a heated argument. Charlie grabbed Debbie from behind and started choking her. Debbie's mother intervened, running up behind Charlie and yelling at him. Debbie's mother told Charlie to let go of her daughter and threatened to kill him if he did not. He let go just as Debbie's brother David came into the room. Debbie's mother said Charlie was trying to kill Debbie. David told Charlie they were "taking it outside." As they started for the door, Charlie grabbed David from behind. David wrapped his arms around Charlie and threw him off the porch onto the ground. David climbed on top of Charlie, holding him down and asked his mother what he should do with Charlie. Debbie's mother did not respond, so David let Charlie up. Once up, Charlie started swearing at Debbie. David lost his composure and began pushing Charlie. After several pushes, Charlie ran away from the house. He returned a few minutes later. From outside the house on the street, he yelled out that he was sorry and began crying. David let him go and he took off in his car. The next day, Charlie told Debbie he was sorry and swore he would never hit her again. Debbie believed him and kept on seeing him.

As time went on, Charlie did not keep his word. He continued to beat Debbie, but never when her family was around. Debbie felt that Charlie never really acted the way a man should. Charlie had no qualms about beating Debbie or her kids, yet when a man confronted Charlie, he was always a coward. When together with Debbie, Charlie often changed jobs. He worked for U-need-A, Can-Go, Mission Trucks, and Enterprise Trucking. Charlie got a new job every few months, leaving him unemployed part of the time. Finances were often tight, generating arguments between Debbie and Charlie.

When Charlie told Debbie he was divorcing Patricia, he told Debbie he loved her and wanted to marry her. Debbie accepted his proposal, but no wedding date was set. After their engagement Charlie returned to driving at Can-Go trucking. Charlie wanted to pick up his payroll check and asked Debbie to ride on the back of his motorcycle. When they arrived, Charlie went inside the office. He came out in only a few minutes. He was really angry. Charlie's boss fired him for coming to work with Debbie. Whenever Charlie beat her, Debbie would ask what she had done wrong. Charlie always told her, to just shut up and take his beating.

In early July 1982, Debbie learned that Charlie's divorce from Patricia was final. She learned that Patricia was letting Charlie stay in his trailer on Patricia's parents' property.

A few days after his divorce from Patricia, Charlie called Debbie on the phone while she was working. He announced that he wanted to marry her. He told Debbie to pick up her kids and drive to Angleton. He said they would get married by a justice of the peace. Debbie was hesitant, but drove to Angleton as Charlie asked. She parked in the courthouse lot. Charlie drove up shortly thereafter. He told Debbie's kids to wait in the car. They went into the courthouse and got married in a mere twenty minutes. After the ceremony, Charlie went back to work. That same day, Debbie and her children moved into Charlie's trailer.

Never needing a reason, Charlie continued to beat Debbie. Charlie, she believed, just loved to hurt her. Not long after getting married, Charlie began beating Debbie's son and daughter, also for no reason. One night, Charlie was so intoxicated that he took out his 22-caliber pistol, removing all but one bullet. He began playing

Russian roulette, spinning the cylinder and pointing the gun at Debbie and her kids. Charlie pulled the trigger, and when the gun did not go off, he told them they would live for now. Debbie and her children were terrified and didn't understand what Charlie was doing.

Debbie never called the police when Charlie beat her, because she had an outstanding arrest warrant for theft by checks. Charlie knew about the warrant and threatened to turn her in if she ever called the police. He added that he would kill her children while she was in jail.

Debbie's recalled that one day, soon after they married, Debbie, the kids and Charlie were visiting Debbie's mother. The police came to their house looking for Debbie while they were away. They searched Charlie's house and found his 22-caliber pistol. They took the pistol, which worried Charlie. He told Debbie, "I have to get the gun back right away." But for some reason Charlie never contacted the police asking about getting his gun back.

Just after Debbie and Charlie got married, two men repossessed his trailer. He had not been making the payments after losing his job at Can-Go Trucking. The men were getting ready to haul away the trailer when they found that the trailer could not be removed without first cutting down a tree. Charlie called Patricia and told her a tree needed to be cut down to get his trailer off the lot. Patricia came over almost immediately and made a deal with the men. They left for the day. Charlie was resigned to the loss of his trailer. He told Debbie they were going to move to Medina County and live in his grandparents' house on 187 acres. His grandparents had passed away and the home was vacant.

Before the family moved to Medina County Charlie got drunk and went through another violent rage. He started beating Debbie, punching her in the face and kicking her with his cowboy boots. Debbie's brother, just happened to come over as Charlie was still beating Debbie. Charlie saw David driving up and ran out the back door of his trailer. When Debbie came to the door her nose was bleeding from Charlie's punches. Enraged, David chased Charlie all over the neighborhood, but could not catch him. During the chase, David yelled at Charlie that he had better get out of town. Charlie yelled back that he was leaving town and moving to San Antonio. David asked Debbie if she was going to move away with Charlie. She said that she was. David got very angry and told her that he would no longer help her out. David said, "If you are stupid enough to stay with Charlie, you are on your own".

The very next day, they loaded up their car and hooked up Debbie's small travel trailer. Debbie drove the Chevrolet truck along with the children. Charlie drove his motorcycle. The family relocated to Medina County.

Charlie's grandparents' home is located just outside of Devine, Texas. For the first few weeks in Devine, Charlie was on his good behavior. Charlie's parents visited often, and he didn't want them to see Debbie beat up. Charlie's parents treated Debbie well when they first met. On her son's twelfth birthday, Charlie's father gave her son a 22-caliber rifle. Charlie's dad and mother pitched in and bought her son a little motor scooter.

Only a few weeks after moving to Devine, Charlie's parents seemed to change their opinion of Debbie and the kids. Iona out of the blue would call the children names. When Iona saw a marijuana leaf tattoo on Debbie's hand, she told Debbie she was trashy and a drug addict. Charlie's parents began treating Debbie and her kids like outcasts.

It was clear to Debbie that Charlie was a mama's boy. Iona always worried about him, while at the same time; his father did not appear to care for his son. Charlie and his father never talked, and Charlie Sr. always frowned when he looked at Charlie Jr.

Life in Devine grew worse for Debbie and her children. Charlie got drunk daily, which led to constant beatings for Debbie and the children. Debbie's daughter was nearly nine when Charlie would roughhouse with her. She often screamed that Charlie had touched her breasts and crotch, while Charlie insisted it was an accident. Charlie made it a point to be in the room when the girl would take a bath. Today, Debbie believes Charlie may have been molesting her daughter. She said her children would not tell her all that had happened. She recalls seeing Charlie coming out of the bedroom with her daughter, who was upset and crying. Debbie blamed her lack of action on her own heavy drinking and being drunk much of the time. In retrospect, Debbie feels extremely sorry for failing to get her children away from Charlie. She feels that she failed to protect her children from a very bad man. The children knew it was hard on her to live with Charlie. She believes her daughter did not tell her all that Charlie was doing to protect the family. She believes her daughter must have some ugly secrets. Debbie told me that her daughter grew up with a drug problem and has problems holding a job. Debbie talks to her daughter all the time, but believes she won't share what may have happened. Debbie now believes that Charlie molested her daughter, but doesn't want her mother to know the truth. Debbie's daughter told her mother that Charlie warned her he would plow her into the fields if she messed with him. He told her he would get a "Pop and Johnny" John Deer tractor and bury her and her mother in the fields on the family farm if she did not obey his wishes. He always added that; "no one would ever find them".

Debbie remembers the day Charlie admitted to getting away with killing a girl when he was a teenager. Charlie said the new sheriff of Medina County accused him but could never prove it. Charlie told Debbie; "Just remember that." It was strange the way he said this to her. He stood there glaring at her. She took the way he said this as a threat. It was as if he was saying, "I got away with murder before so don't mess with me." In the year or so the family was living in Medina County, Debbie would occasionally leave Charlie after a beating. She would return in a day or two. She always came back to him, but admits she does not know why.

The end of the marriage came on a very cold day. The family was driving back from Hondo. Charlie made Debbie's children sit in the pickup truck bed, while Charlie rolled up the windows and turned on the heater. Debbie opened the window and asked her children if they were okay. Charlie went ballistic. He yelled at her to roll the window up. Debbie did not act fast enough for Charlie and he reached behind her, grabbing a plastic gun rack that hung on the window frame. He pulled the rack off and began choking her with it. Debbie almost lost conscience. She feels that Charlie almost killed her that time. Debbie thought for sure Charlie would continue beating her and that she was going to die that day.

When they got home Debbie made dinner and waited until Charlie passed out in bed. The kids were doing their homework when she said she finally had it with Charlie. Debbie told her son to go outside and disable Charlie's motorcycle so he could not follow them. Her son pulled out all the wires so the motorcycle would not run. They grabbed some clothes and got into the truck. Her son took the 22-caliber rifle that Charlie's father gave him and he sat in the truck bed, holding the rifle over the tailgate. Debbie told her son to shoot Charlie if he started after them. He told his mother not to worry, that he would shoot Charlie if he chased them. When they got to the livestock gate, Debbie opened it and threw away the key. Out of spite, she left the gate open so all the cows grazing on the farm could get out. Debbie drove straight to San Leon and to her mother's house that night.

A few weeks later, Charlie's attorney called Debbie. He told her that Charlie wanted a divorce. Debbie told the lawyer that she had no objections to the divorce whatsoever. The lawyer was extremely concerned about the 22-caliber rifle given to her son by Charlie. He told her she needed to return the rifle in exchange her belongings left behind at the family home. She did not understand why Charlie wanted the rifle back.

They made arrangements to meet the lawyer at Charlie's parents' home in Hondo. Debbie arranged to have some male friends go with her to retrieve her travel trailer and belongings. When they arrived in Hondo, Charlie and his parents were at the house. Debbie looked at Charlie Sr. and Iona, who appeared angry, but to her surprise they said nothing to her. Charlie Jr. never spoke except to ask where the rifle was. She handed the rifle to Charlie.

Debbie and her friends followed Charlie Senior and they all drove out to the grandparents' home. Someone had filled a trailer up with their belongings.

Debbie's friends hooked up the travel trailer and she left. Much to Debbie's disbelief, Charlie Jr. did not make a scene that day. She never saw Charlie again and learned he died some years later. When she learned he died; she felt a great relief.

Charlie's Seventh Marriage: Sherry Yates "Drinking and Lying"

In May or June 1985, Charlie was living in La Coste, Texas. He was still in the process of divorcing Deborah Biggs. Charlie drove into Devine to purchase gas at a Citgo station with a small convenience store. The cashier on duty was Sherry Yates. Sherry was a single mother in her mid-twenties, raising a young boy. Sherry was 5'2" tall and 105 pounds with shoulder-length brown hair. Sherry's marriage to Ricky Yates, a Medina County boy, had ended. She was originally from Indiana and had no family in Texas. Sherry talked about her short marriage to Charlie Hitzfelder Jr., whom she thought was a good-looking man and generally very nice to her.

Charlie asked her out on a few dates. They seemed to get along well. At first, Charlie appeared to be a caring man. He treated her eighteen-month-old son well. After a few dates, Charlie asked her to marry him. Sherry was struggling financially and did not have a place to stay. She thought Charlie would be okay to live with. She was desperate to put food on the table for her son. She told Charlie she would marry him, but insisted he be faithful to her. Charlie told her he was a one-woman man and that he would never stray. They drove to Crystal City in Zavala County to get married by a justice of the peace. There was no marriage celebration involved.

During the first month of the marriage, they got along well. Charlie introduced Sherry to his sister, Jeanette. Sherry also met Charlie's mother, Iona, and his father, Charlie Sr. It was apparent Iona really cared for Charlie. On the other hand, Charlie and his dad did not get along. There was tension between them. She thought his dad did not care to be around Charlie.

Almost immediately after they got married Charlie started drinking heavily. He was drunk most of the time. Sherry also suspected that he was seeing a woman in San Antonio. He would come home late at night drunk. She could smell perfume on his clothing. Charlie lied to her constantly. He lied about everything. He lied about money, where he had been, whom he had been with, and other things. She could not trust him from the beginning of their relationship. Charlie was not physically violent to her. He did not hit Sherry with his fists but did throw things at her. However, he was verbally abusive. He would call her names, for little or no reason. It was clear that he did not respect Sherry.

One afternoon, Sherry finally accused Charlie of cheating on her. He denied seeing any other women, but she knew he was lying. His drinking and his lies got worse. Charlie would stay out all night, returning home drunk early in the morning. The nights he did stay home, Sherry heard him talking in his sleep. Charlie would have nightmares and wake up screaming, frightening Sherry and her son. When Charlie left for work, he always carried his 38-caliber revolver with him. He told Sherry the gun was for protection. She was afraid of him when he handled that gun, because he was drunk all the time.

One day he told Sherry that his father was the county sheriff for twenty years. For some reason he also told Sherry her he was accused of killing a girl he dated when he was a teenager. When Charlie told her the story, she was very frightened. The way he told the story scared Sherry even more. It was as if he was proud of being was accused of a murder. After that, Sherry was constantly afraid that Charlie would get drunk and hurt someone. His lies and drinking were just too much for her. She finally decided that being married to Charlie was not a very good idea. They were only married four or five months when she decided to leave Charlie. One day when he was at work, she packed up her belongings and moved back to Indiana. She did not tell did tell Charlie she was leaving; fearing what he might do to her. She never saw Charlie again. Sherry said she eventually divorced Charlie, but could not remember where she got the divorce. While they were married, Charlie drove a brown-over-orange Lincoln.

ELEVEN
"Charlie Was Quite The Gentleman"
Charlie's Eighth Marriage: Faye Bokkean

Charlie moved to the Casa Grande area of Arizona in late 1989. He worked as a long-haul truck driver for Werner Enterprises based in Iowa. Charlie was driving an eighteen-wheeler, making runs from the West Coast to Florida and the East Coast to Canada. Werner Enterprises is a nationwide trucking company. Charlie held this job from October 9, 1989 until April 22, 1991.

Charlie was getting ready to head to the West Coast with a load of dry goods. Before leaving Casa Grande, he fueled his rig at a truck stop. Truck Stops of America is located just outside of Casa Grande. Casa Grande is a small city near the junction of I-10 and I-8, fifty miles south of Phoenix, Arizona. This stop is on a major route for long-haul truckers working the southern corridor.

At the truck stop, Charlie met a cashier named Faye Bokkean. He befriended forty-year-old Faye, who had been married a few times before, but was now single and not dating. Faye was the mother of a nineteen-year-old daughter and a twenty-two-year-old son. Faye was originally from West Virginia but lived in Casa Grande after ending a relationship. Charlie and Faye dated a few times over the next year. When Charlie was in Casa Grande, he would take Faye out on dates before he left on a trip.

One year into dating Faye, Charlie called her from Southern California. He told Faye he was headed to Las Vegas and asked her to meet him there. He said he wanted to get married. Charlie knew that Faye's son was engaged and expressed an interest to get married in Las Vegas. Charlie told her that both couples could get married at the same time. Faye believed Charlie was a nice guy. She was having a hard time financially and thought his income would help. Faye admits she did not love Charlie, but thought he was harmless. Faye liked the idea of a double wedding. She immediately said yes to Charlie's proposal. Charlie told them to meet him at a Las Vegas truck stop. They met him on September 9, 1991. Charlie, Faye, Faye's son, and his fiancée were married in civil ceremonies at one of the drive-through wedding chapels in Las Vegas.

Soon after they got married, Charlie asked Faye if she wanted to join him driving around the country on the open road. Charlie told Faye the trip would only last a few weeks. At first, Faye thought riding around the country would be fun, so she jumped at the chance. To her dismay, two weeks turned into two months. They traveled all around the United States and Canada. They slept in the truck's sleeper compartment. When they finally returned to Casa Grande, Faye was happy to get off the road. She moved in with her son and his new wife, living in an apartment in Arizona City, Arizona. Charlie was on the road much of the time, so Faye and Charlie got along pretty well.

Six months into the marriage, Charlie told her that he decided to quit his job and move back to Texas. Faye believes he may have gotten fired, but he never said why he stopped working for Werner. Charlie called his sister, Jeanette, and asked if they could stay with her and her husband in Castroville. Jeanette agreed, so they loaded up their belongings and moved to Texas. Jeanette doted over Charlie. She had married a local man of German descent.

After Charlie and Faye moved in, Charlie started looking for work in San Antonio. When Charlie stopped working for Werner, the only transportation the couple had was a beat-up Ford Pinto. Soon after moving to Texas, Charlie found a job at a San Antonio warehouse. But he only held this job for a few months.

Charlie came home from work one day and was excited over a job he found, driving for Olmos Construction. After a few months on this job, Charlie was promoted to a working supervisor. Now that Charlie was a supervisor, he was provided with a company pickup truck. Charlie was able to drive the truck to and from San

Antonio. Faye finally had the Pinto to drive to the store and other places she needed to visit. After a few months, Charlie traded in the Pinto for a Ford Thunderbird. For a short while, they were doing well financially. A few months after landing the job with Olmos, Charlie found a double-wide mobile home to rent. It was located on FM 471, which is the road from Castroville to Natalia.

Faye had problems finding a job close to home because Castroville was a small town.

She was very bored, lonely, and unhappy living in Texas. Charlie was at work all day, while she was without friends or the opportunity to meet people. They lived way out in the country and there were not many people around. About eighteen months into the marriage, Faye's daughter Tina called. She was single, twenty-one, and was raising two small babies on her own. She had no where to go. Faye spoke to Charlie, and he agreed to let Tina and the babies stay with them.

Even after her daughter and grand children moved in, she still was still unhappy living in Texas.

Faye said Charlie got along well with his sister Jeanette. She knew he had another sister, Barbara, but she never met her.

In 1992, Charlie's mother became very sick. Before long, Charlie got a call that his mom had passed away. Charlie and Faye went to the family home in Hondo for her funeral service. Nearly one hundred people attended the service. After Charlie's mother died, Charlie Junior was withdrawn for awhile. Charlie took long walks to think about things. Faye would join Charlie on the walks. After his mother's passing, Charlie and Faye visited his father a few times, but the visits were short. Charlie and his dad didn't talk much. There always seemed to be tension between the two.

When the author spoke to Faye, she did not know that Charlie had children from his previous relationships. Charlie never talked about them, apparently keeping his earlier life a secret. Charlie told Faye that he was married "two or three times." She had no idea that Charlie had been married seven times before marrying her. Faye recalled Charlie mentioning a woman named Juanita. He treated Faye well during their time together. Charlie was always a gentleman to her. He never hit her, but they argued about money and her dislike for living in Texas. A few months before she left Charlie, They moved from the double wide trailer located on FM 471. Charlie rented a small single-wide trailer in Natalia. They moved into the trailer, even though it was much smaller than the double-wide they occupied. Charlie told her money was the reason they had to move. Faye was not working and Charlie had many bills.

Charlie and Faye would go out to a bar once in awhile and have a few drinks. Occasionally, they went out to dinner. While together, Charlie always came home right after work. Charlie drank whiskey occasionally and chain-smoked cigarettes. Faye never saw Charlie use drugs. After Faye left Charlie, her daughter told her that Charlie used "speed" or ephedrine pills to stay awake when driving his truck. Charlie never abused Faye, either physical or mentally. He was actually very nice to Faye. Charlie did not engage in any peculiar sexual habits with Faye.

Faye said she never knew Charlie was once a suspect in Carolyn Covey's murder. When told of this, she seemed shocked. She said Charlie never had a pistol when driving a truck, although she never looked for one. She remembers Charlie owning a 22-caliber rifle during their marriage. Faye said she left Charlie because she was unhappy, often arguing over money. Money issues and Faye's disdain for Texas brought an end to the marriage. She finally decided the Texas lifestyle was not for her and moved to Oklahoma, where she had family. When she left, Faye took Charlie's gray 1978 Ford Thunderbird. After settling in Oklahoma, she filed for divorce. The court sent Charlie the divorce papers, and Charlie signed them. A few months later, their divorce was finalized. After Faye left Texas, she never saw Charlie again.

Charlie's Ninth "Common Law" Marriage: Dolly Stevens-Buser, "I Felt Sorry For Him"

Dolly Buser was Charlie's last companion in life. Charlie met Dolly through her uncle, who worked with Charlie at Olmos Construction and Trucking in San Antonio. At the time they met, Charlie was living in a single-wide trailer located in Natalia, a small Medina County community. Charlie told Dolly's uncle he wanted to see the rodeo in San Antonio. Dolly's uncle knew his niece also liked rodeos. Neither Charlie nor Dolly was dating at the time, so a meeting was arranged. When they met, they seemed to get along. They never made it to the rodeo, but continued seeing each other. Eventually Dolly moved into Charlie's trailer on Bartlett Street in Natalia. Dolly's pregnant twenty-two-year-old daughter also moved in with them.

Charlie treated Dolly fairly well during their relationship. She said he did not have friends and was a loner. Charlie often went to a local club, the Horseshoe Inn, to play pool and drink. He also frequented the Last Call bar on FM 410. To this day, Dolly feels certain Charlie was having an affair with a customer there named Betty. Charlie never beat or mistreated Dolly. She reported that Charlie was very meek and timid. She referred to him as a "skinny little wimp." For the most part, Charlie was subservient to Dolly. However, when he got drunk, and that was often, he became a totally different person. Charlie would talk badly about people, prompting Dolly to quickly put him in his place. He would back down. Charlie chain-smoked cigarettes and loved Jack Daniel's whiskey and beer. Charlie thought he had a policeman's mentality, often dressing like a cop. Dolly thought Charlie acted this way because his father had been sheriff. Charlie never had anything nice to say about people, and spent a lot of time reading old books, like Louie Lamoure novels. He also liked wood carving as a hobby. Dolly said Charlie was never physically abusive to her or her children. He never made sexual advances to her daughters.

Dolly was aware that Charlie was a suspect in the 1961 murder of Carolyn Covey. She remembered Charlie often talking about Carolyn Covey. Charlie told her one day that he "beat that case." As Charlie told Dolly the story, he smiled and laughed. This seemed strange to Dolly. She recalls Charlie receiving a letter from a woman, asking him to tell the truth about the death of her daughter. When Charlie read the letter, he just laughed, throwing it away. Charlie often told Dolly about his marriage to Juanita and what a good woman she was. Charlie also talked about another marriage to a pothead who was always in trouble. Charlie told her the woman's children tore up his grandfather's home.

Dolly did not love Charlie. When he got sick, no one in his family stepped forward to help him. She stayed with Charlie when he learned he was going to die. From the day she met Charlie, he complained about a pain in his stomach. Charlie had not been to a doctor to check it out. Dolly finally got Charlie to see her family doctor, who administered a battery of tests. The doctor told Charlie he had colon cancer and needed surgery. Charlie was devastated when he first heard the news. He had two surgeries, but neither helped much. The doctor finally told Charlie he was going to die. Charlie confided that he did not want to die alone.

At first, Charlie stayed in the hospital. The doctors eventually told him there was nothing more they could do and sent him home. Charlie ended up in bed in his small trailer. Towards the end of life, Charlie wore a colostomy bag, and soon after that a urine draining bag. Charlie was in severe pain for months, slowly withering away. The doctors gave Charlie powerful painkillers, like morphine, but Charlie was in pain all the time. It took months for him to die. Social security benefits helped with expenses. After a few months at home, Charlie would not eat and was growing very thin. The doctor gave him baby food through a feeding tube. As death approached, Charlie talked about where he would be buried. Charlie told Dolly he was a Navy veteran of the Vietnam War. Charlie decided to be buried at Fort Sam Houston National Cemetery.

Once in a while, Charlie's sister Jeanette visited him. Charlie had no friends, and pretty much died alone. Charlie's Uncle Amos lived in Medina County and they visited him a few times before he was too ill to travel. Dolly could tell Uncle Amos did not care much for Charlie. There was tension between them. Dolly wondered why Charlie went to his house. Charlie's relationships with his two sisters, Jeanette and Barbara, were awkward. Charlie was angry with Barbara for the way she handled their father's estate after he died. Charlie complained that Barbara took all the good stuff and left him nothing. Charlie had nothing to do with her after this.

Toward the end of his life, Charlie was pretty much sleeping all the time. He was always in pain. Finally, Charlie just stopped breathing and died. Dolly called the sheriff and they sent out the justice of the peace. The funeral home people took Charlie's body away. Only Charlie's sisters and one of his daughters attended the service Dolly arranged for him. Thirty of Dolly's family members attended the funeral. Charlie wanted to be buried in his cowboy boots and have his cowboy hat in his casket. He did not want to be embalmed and asked to be buried a pine box. Charlie's last wishes were honored by Dolly. She had to borrow money to pay for the service and the funeral director. Charlie's family did not help with any of the expenses. Charlie was taken to San Antonio and laid to rest. Dolly bought Charlie's trailer from its owner after Charlie died. Charlie left behind a few personal effects, including a wristwatch purchased by Dolly, a Chevrolet S-10 pickup, his clothes, and a 22-caliber rifle, which Dolly still keeps in her bedroom.

The rifle is a Remington 22-caliber, short, single-shot, bolt-action rifle. The gun is operational, but in poor shape. There was no serial number visible on the weapon.

Charlie also owned a pistol, which Dolly revealed he always carried when on the road. According to Dolly, Charlie either pawned the gun when money got tight or sold it to someone at Olmos Construction. Dolly was unaware that several girls were murdered with a 22-caliber firearm and a 38-caliber revolver.

Domestic Violence
Why Did These Women Stay With Charlie?

Domestic violence is a sad fact in some relationships. When Charlie grew up, domestic violence often went unreported. Women were often afraid to come forward. Most states did not have domestic violence laws on the books in the 1960s. The police were rarely involved in incidents, and when called to a house, they calmed the situation down and left without making arrests. In retrospect, the way law enforcement handled domestic violence was an embarrassment. Violence breeds violence, increasing the incidence of physical abuse. Perpetrators become emboldened when nothing is done to them. It was a dirty secret in society that a man could physically and mentally abuse his spouse and get away with in. Generations of women grew up in families where their fathers physically abused their mothers. The cycle of abuse and acceptance was, and still is, passed on. Many of the women Charlie abused came from homes where their fathers often beat their mothers. It's easy to understand how these women could accept Charlie's terrible physical abuse and stay with him. Fortunately, many states have passed laws requiring an aggressor be arrested on the spot. Restraining orders are often mandated. Even if a woman does not want her husband or boyfriend arrested, the police have no choice. Today there is help for victims of domestic violence.

TWELVE
Checking Out Charlie

In February 1980, the author, tried to determine Charlie Juniors possible involvement in the "skeletal remains" case in Manvel, Texas. Sheriff Butch Campsey made another extended visit to Brazoria County in late February 1980. The sheriff and author devised a plan hoping to gather information connecting Charlie to the unknown remains. To us, the similarity of the Carolyn Covey murder and my case "had" to be connected.

Campsey completed more research on Charlie Hitzfelder. The Galveston Sheriff's Department revealed Charlie had been picked up a few times, mostly for traffic violations and once for drunk driving. Charlie's wife, Juanita Lamb Hitzfelder, died unexpectedly only one month before. The Galveston County Coroner's office reported that Juanita was forty-two when she died. Charlie took Juanita to Memorial Hospital on January 13, 1980. She apparently suffered a heart attack. Charlie Jr. was by her side and refused to let anyone, including Juanita's own daughter visit with her. The next morning, Juanita suffered a second, perhaps third, heart attack and died. This information was of particular interest. The Galveston County Coroner performed an autopsy on Juanita. When admitted to the hospital, she was listed as having an "acute myocardial infarction with heart block and cardiogenic shock." The cause of her death was listed as "acute myocardial infarction, posteroseptal wall." In layman's terms, Juanita suffered a heart attack.

A few days later, a copy of the autopsy report completed by Dr. Iver Diaz, M.D. was received. Some of the comments were particularly interesting under the section titled: Clinical Summary.

"This 41-year-old white woman was brought by her husband to the ER of Memorial Hospital of Galveston County on January 13, 1980, at 3:40 P.M. She was in critical condition, had several hours history of chest pain, and syncopal episode at home. In the emergency room, she was found dusky, sweaty, and groggy. There was bradycardial with soft heart sounds. ECG showed pattern of inferior myocardial infarction with third-degree heart block. Following frequent PVCs, her blood pressure soon dropped to impalpable and she became comatose, responding only to pain. A variety of drugs were used in the emergency room, including Atropine, Xylocaine, Decadron, Aramine, etc. The patient was taken to Catheterization Laboratory for insertion of temporary pacemaker. This patient had a very complicated short hospital course. Her blood pressure was restored with Dopamine and there was return to endogenous cardiac rhythm. Later the same day, she was awakened and able to communicate. Subsequently, she suffered generalized seizure disorder, developed erratic cardiac rhythm with recurrent ventricular fibrillation, all terminated by CPR. The following morning, she was awake and responsive, but her blood pressure was unobtainable and both pupils were dilated. Soon she developed severe ventricular fibrillation and cardio respiratory arrest. CPR was instituted unsuccessfully. She was pronounced dead on January 14, 1980 at 8:48 A.M."

Juanita's autopsy report had the following comments: "Enzyme studies and EKG changes were 'suggestive' of a heart attack. There were no inflammatory changes on the anterior wall of the heart. There were no gross changes of myocardial infarction seen at the time of the autopsy. Finally, Juanita's coronary arteries were narrowed, but patent. One more thing of interest was included in the report. Dr. Diaz wrote that he felt 'the husband is more than normally concerned about the cause of death."

According to Dr. Diaz of the Galveston County Coroner's office, testing prior to Juanita's death was indicative of a person having a heart attack. However, his examination did not take into consideration possible other causes of death. He had no reason to suspect foul play. Juanita could have died some other way, because the doctor did not look for other causes of death. He did not examine her tissues for other possibilities, such as poisoning. Dr. Diaz was told Juanita had been treated in the ER for a possible heart attack. His examination was based on this fact. The possibility of foul play remained. Tissue samples from Juanita's body had been kept by the coroner. The coroner was asked to place a hold on the tissue samples until further investigation was completed. Dr. Diaz said he would make sure the samples were kept viable. Sheriff Campsey knew that more than a few people connected to Charlie and his father died of so-called heart attacks. Many people connected to the Covey murder died very young and the cause of death always seemed to be a heart attack. As an investigator, Sheriff Campsey suggested the possibility of some kind of poisoning of these people, who died suddenly and unexpectedly, had to be considered.

Sheriff Campsey, by now was getting more grief from the county commissioners for reopening the Carolyn Covey murder. As an elected official, they could not tell him what to do, but they could refuse to pay the bills. They saw it as a fool's errand for him to come to Galveston and Brazoria counties on a nineteen-year-old murder. Charlie Hitzfelder Sr. still had a few friends in county government, but this was not going to stop Sheriff Campsey. If he had to pay his travel expenses and investigate on his days off he would. The sheriff said he would be back to Brazoria County as soon as he could.

As it turned out, Butch Campsey did pay for many trips to Brazoria County. The county commissioners refused to allocate money for what they considered a waste of time. On one trip, Butch had to borrow gas money to drive to Brazoria County. He was so broke he would buy a loaf of bread and a package of baloney for the trip. When in Brazoria County, Butch, Frank Perkins or Deputy Bill Butler would sleep on Detective Skarka's couch or floor. The Covey murder investigation was done on the cheap. Adding intrigue to the situation, Detective Skarka could not reveal to his supervisor what he was up to, because no time was allowed to investigate this case. Detective Skarka was flatly told he had more pressing things to do, such as solving the thefts from oil rigs, oil fields, and other burglaries. These crimes were more important to his supervisors. Many times he tried to convince supervisors that there was a viable suspect in Charlie Hitzfelder Jr. This was all to no avail. When the subject of the Manvel case was mentioned, the response was that "there was no crime in Manvel." There was no murder, only found bones.

Skarka and Campsey were convinced that Charles Joseph Hitzfelder Jr. warranted further investigation. Butch came to Brazoria County with Bill Butler in April 1980. That afternoon, Charlie's trailer inside the Lazy Wasp Trailer Park was placed under surveillance. Charlie was between wives as far as investigators knew. Many years later it was learned that Charlie was involved with Patricia Sweet-Ellis. That evening before dark, Charlie's car was parked in the trailer park. A little after the surveillance began, Charlie drove alone, slowly out of the trailer park. Charlie drove a few miles south on Highway 6 to Grace Memorial Park Cemetery. He drove onto the grounds, parked his car and walked through the maze of headstones up to a new gravesite. With the aid of binoculars, investigators could see Charlie talking. He was either talking to himself or to this unknown grave. Charlie was quite animated as he spoke, making gestures with his arms and hands as he stood there. For the next twenty-five minutes, he talked non-stop. Even to police investigators, this was a little spooky.

After Charlie finished his chat with the dead, he returned to his car and drove straight back to his trailer. Investigators could not contain themselves. They had to see who he was talking to. They drove back to the cemetery and got out of the car. The investigators walked to the spot where they had seen Charlie standing. The headstone Charlie was talking to was Juanita Lamb Hitzfelder's. The headstone read: Juanita Hitzfelder, Born 1939, and Died January 14, 1980. Next to her name was Charles Joseph Hitzfelder Jr., August 12, 1942. There was a space to the left of Charlie's name for his date of death. Charlie's actions were just plain weird. All of the investigators concluded that Charlie Hitzfelder Jr. was at the very least a little strange.

It did not take much more investigating to conclude Charlie was worth looking into a deeper. After looking at Juanita's headstone, they drove back to Charlie's trailer and continued surveillance. For several hours, they sat waiting for Charlie to leave the house. Around 10 PM, Charlie was still inside his trailer. Investigators knew he was inside because one walked by the trailer and heard the radio playing a Merle Haggard song. Someone could be heard walking around inside. They felt certain that Charlie was inside and did not leave the trailer.

On the way back to Brazoria County, the investigators discussed what they witnessed that night. They wondered if they could plant a listening device at Juanita's grave. Investigators thought Charlie might be telling Juanita he was sorry for killing her. After the surveillance, investigators were able to interest Lt. Eddie Barr of the Galveston County Sheriff's Department Crime Task Force in the case. Eddie considered Charlie Hitzfelder Jr. a possible suspect. Now retired, Eddie Barr spends his time at his home away from home, the Galveston Yacht Club. Eddie remembers Charlie Hitzfelder Jr. and believes today that Charlie was responsible for some of the murders. Eddie Barr recalled some of his efforts to connect the dots to Charlie. He investigated several connections. Eddie spent many hours investigating Charlie but could never make a case against him. He learned from Sheriff Campsey and I that Charlie was talking to Juanita's grave. Eddie arranged to place a bug on the headstone. Charlie continued to visit her grave regularly, while Eddie watched Charlie talking to Juanita's headstone.

The bug only picked up low mumbling, so investigators never learned what he was saying. As time passed, other crimes and murders had to be investigated. Around 1984 or 1985, Eddie heard that Charlie moved from the Galveston area. This put an end to Eddie's investigative efforts into Charlie Hitzfelder Jr.

Charlie Jr. Takes and Passes a Polygraph

In 1981, Sheriff Campsey spent all of his free time in the pursuit of justice for Carolyn Covey. By now, he considered Charlie Hitzfelder Jr. a good suspect. This opinion was based on many factors. Butch looked into similar Galveston and Brazoria crimes. He had tracked down and re-interviewed many of the original witnesses from 1961. One such witness was Dennis Heyen, who had seen Charlie Hitzfelder Jr. and Carolyn Covey together at the gas station where he worked the day before Carolyn went missing. Dennis shared this information with Sheriff Charlie months before her body was found.

There was also the Hondo resident who recalled Charlie Jr. being in town around the time of Carolyn's disappearance. This was very interesting to Sheriff Campsey, and he began to devote more of his free time to the Covey murder. He let the newspapers know the Covey case had been reopened. Reacting to a newspaper story in the Hondo Anvil, former Sheriff Charlie Hitzfelder Sr. called Butch and asked the sheriff why he was pursuing his son. Campsey told the old sheriff that it was because Junior's name kept coming up during his investigation. Butch tried to explain to Charlie Sr. that there was nothing personal in reopening the Covey case. He told Charlie Sr. that the question of his son being a suspect could be easily cleared up if Charlie Jr. took a polygraph test. Charlie Sr. said he would look into this and get back to him.

About two months later, Butch received a letter from a Houston area private-for-hire polygraph examiner. The letter alleged that Charles Hitzfelder Jr. took and passed a polygraph test on July 2, 1981. The test was administered at the polygraph examiner's office in Houston. The report was suspect. Case information was submitted by Charles Hitzfelder Sr. The examiner's written report implied that standard polygraph methods utilizing relevant, irrelevant, and control question techniques were utilized on each test chart. The polygraph examiner concluded that the test subject, Charles Hitzfelder Jr., was being truthful when he took and passed the polygraph test regarding the murder of Carolyn Covey. Butch immediately realized that there were several problems with this polygraph test. The biggest problem was Charlie Hitzfelder Sr. hiring his own polygraph examiner. Next problem was the fact that Charlie Sr. provided the case information. Charlie Sr. was also present during the polygraph test. This fact alone was extremely unorthodox. It was also disclosed that the test failed to note who put together the test questions; also a suspicious way for a professional examiner to operate. The letter to Butch did not include test questions or poly-grams charts Finally, and most glaringly, was the examiner's statement that in his professional opinion the subject was being truthful when answering relevant questions. Butch wondered how Charlie Jr. could have been found to be telling the truth after reviewing the examiner's questions.

One question had a glaring inconsistency:

Question #5:
Did your mother arrive in San Diego on February 15, like you said?
Answer: Yes

According to the examiner, this question was answered truthfully by Charlie Jr. However, the Hitzfelders previously reported that Charlie's mother left Hondo on February 14, driving Charlie's car. Mary Ruth Cadenhead said the trip to San Diego took three days. She rode with Charlie's mother. Mary Ruth recalled that February 14 was her father's birthday and she was still in Hondo to help celebrate. They left Hondo on February 15 and would not have arrived in San Diego until at least February 18, 1961.

The examiner's report also indicated that Charlie Hitzfelder Sr. told the polygraph examiner that his wife left Hondo in Charlie's car the morning of February 14, 1961. Inconsistencies such as this are among the reasons polygraph tests are not admissible in U.S. criminal courts. There is too much room for interpretations. There is also a widespread belief that a polygraph operator can be bought and paid for. A polygraph is only a tool that may suggest deception by an examinee. A good examiner can use deception by the examinee as a means to get a person to tell the truth.

Sheriff Campsey Fights the Good Fight For the Next Decade

Butch Campsey continued to do the best he could investigating Charlie Hitzfelder Jr. possible involvement in the death of Claudette Carolyn Covey. He was still faced with county commissioners who did not want him looking into the Covey murder. Butch had a growing family to support, and any investigating had to be paid for out of his own pocket. Butch Campsey served two terms as Medina County Sheriff. In 1987, he was elected Medina county judge and served eight years. All the while, Butch tried to put together the facts from the Covey murder and build a criminal case against Charlie Hitzfelder Jr.

In 1981, it was learned that Charlie had an outstanding warrant for writing bad checks. Butch decided to arrest Charlie for the outstanding warrant. This would give him a chance to meet face-to-face with Charlie Jr. The arrest was coordinated with Eddie Barr and the Galveston County Sheriff's Department. Charlie was picked up at his trailer one evening.

Charlie had married Patricia Sweet, who had three children from a previous marriage. Eddie Barr knocked on the door of the trailer. After a few minutes, Charlie came to the door and was told there was a warrant for his arrest. Charlie looked surprised, sensing he knew Campsey from somewhere. He asked Campsey what department he was from. Campsey told him he was the sheriff of Medina County. Charlie's facial expression changed instantly. He had a blank look on his face and began to shake. He knew something was up. Charlie told Campsey that he knew that the bad check warrant was being used as an excuse to pick him up so he could be questioned. Charlie was handcuffed and put into Campsey's car.

Before leaving for jail, investigators got permission from Patricia to search the trailer, hoping to find a gun or something that would connect Charlie to the spate of murders. Patricia Sweet was concerned as to why four sheriff deputies came to arrest Charlie on a bad check warrant. Patricia was told that Charlie might be involved in some other illegal activity. The search of the trailer did not find anything of real interest. They found a small amount of marijuana in Charlie's car. There was only a cigarette's worth amount of marijuana, so Charlie was not charged with illegal drug possession. Patricia watched Campsey flush the marijuana down her toilet. The front passenger seat in Charlie's car was not connected to the car's frame. While odd, the sheriff did not think much about it at the time. Later, investigators learned that a girl was recently kidnapped and raped in San Marcos, Texas. The suspect tried to kill the woman. The suspect's car had a disconnected front passenger seat. The suspect also looked very similar to Charlie. Soon after the kidnapping, the San Marcos Police declared that a suspect was under arrest for this crime. They were not interested in talking to Charlie.

Charlie was taken to the Galveston County Sheriff's Department for booking. Charlie was asked if he would talk about the Carolyn Covey murder. Charlie asked why the sheriff had not gotten over the Covey murder. He told Campsey, "You can't prove I was involved." As Charlie said this, he had a smirk on his face, believing he was smarter than anyone in the room. At first, Charlie's arrogance made him willing to speak to investigators. Charlie was taken to a larger meeting room at the sheriff's department.

Unknown to Charlie, Eddie Barr had arranged to spread photos of several young murdered girls around the room. The photos of their bodies were tacked on the wall. Investigators felt Charlie may be involved with some of these murders. Charlie walked into the room and only briefly looked at the photos. He never batted any eye, acting as if there were no photos on the walls. Campsey began talking to Charlie. He sat there stoically, never asking about the photos on the wall. Charlie showed no concern at all. After only a few minutes Charlie asked Campsey why he was taken to the Galveston County Jail for such a minor thing as a bad check warrant. Butch countered that it had been twenty years since Carolyn Covey was murdered. He told Charlie he wanted to talk about her death. Butch could see that Charlie was thinking. For a moment, Butch thought Charlie was going to talk, but instead asked to make his phone call. After the call, Charlie came back into the room and said he had spoken to his father. Charlie's father told him not to talk to anyone. This put an end to the interview. Investigators felt they may never get a chance to talk to Charlie again. Charlie was taken to the booking area and turned over to a deputy for processing. Charlie was left in jail overnight. Patricia Sweet bailed him out the next morning.

Before leaving the Galveston area, Eddie Barr promised to continue trying to connect Charlie to his cases. Campsey was even more determined to look into Charlie's possible involvement in Carolyn's murder.

Keeping Up The Pressure

Over the next year or two, Butch and his deputies made several visits to the Galveston area. Butch checked in with Eddie Barr and other agencies keeping an eye on Charlie. On one of the trips, Butch and Probation Officer Frank Perkins drove to Galveston. The next morning, it was decided to initiate surveillance of Charlie at his job, Can-Go Trucking. Investigators sat outside the company offices in an unmarked police car, watching Charlie's car for several hours. They decided to drive by the front of the company offices. Charlie was working inside, standing at a window, and recognized Sheriff Campsey. Charlie must have learned that Campsey was in the company's parking lot. When they saw he was aware they were outside, they decided that any further surveillance was useless.

They started to drive back to their motel. As they were driving down one of the main roads, three or four Texas City Police cars came up from behind with their red lights flashing. Butch wondered why he was being stopped, but he pulled over. One of the Texas City policemen walked up to the car with his hand on his gun. As other officers got out of their cars, they all drew their service revolvers. They ordered Campsey and Perkins out of the car. One of the policemen leaned the sheriff up against the hood of his car and another pulled Perkins out of the car. The police could see he was a sheriff. He had his badge on and the car had a police radio mounted inside. This made no impression on the officers. They shoved the sheriff around. They spoke to Campsey as if he were a common criminal. One of the officers told Campsey that he knew he was the Medina County Sheriff. The policeman told him bluntly that he had no business in Texas City. It was suggested that Campsey leave town and never come back. As a parting threat the policeman said he had received a call from his chief. The chief told the policeman to tell Campsey to get out of Texas City, or else.

Campsey decided not to argue the point then and there. They were allowed to go. This was a very strange thing to happen. Never before in anyone's memory had a sitting sheriff, driving a county car, been pulled over by local police and threatened. It was learned later that someone of importance called the Texas City Police. This person asked the chief for a favor. The caller said Campsey had been bothering his son at Can-Go Trucking. This was the same kind of influence peddling and intimidation that went on when Sheriff Hitzfelder was in power. Campsey never thought the old sheriff could pull strings after being out of office. It was clear that at the very least, someone wanted to make a point. Whoever arranged this intimidation had political connections high up in the city. It was clear to Campsey that years after Charlie Sr. left office, he still had the political power to intimidate hundreds of miles from Hondo.

THIRTEEN
Young Girls Kidnapped, Raped, and Murdered

In 1971, a killer or killers began an unprecedented series of abductions and murders of young women in southeast Texas. In the next ten years, over forty young girls in the Galveston/Houston area were murdered. The girls were generally between the ages of twelve and sixteen. The physical characteristics of the victims were often very similar, some looking much like Carolyn Covey. All of the victims were Caucasian or Hispanic, except one. Most were approximately 5' to 5'4" tall. Several of the victims had an olive complexion and wore shoulder-length hair.

Many of the girls were found nude with their underwear missing—apparently taken as souvenirs by the killer. These crimes occurred in the southern portions of Harris County, the northern portion of Brazoria County, and throughout Galveston County. Both Galveston County and Brazoria County had victims taken and later found throughout the Houston area. The method of operation was very similar to Carolyn's murder. Their bodies were dumped in fields near highways or near bodies of water. In 1971, there was no such thing as an Amber Alert for missing or abducted children. There were no registry laws such as Megan's Law or Jessica's Law. If a young child went missing, law enforcement's approach was very different than it is today. Often, the missing child was treated as a runaway. In some cases, days or weeks went by before law enforcement began looking for the missing child. Back then, people, including police, didn't recognize the serious nature of these disappearances. No one wanted to believe child predators were on the prowl in their community. The safe and simple life portrayed on television shows like "Leave it to Beaver,"

"Father Knows Best," and the "Ozzie and Harriet Show" were gone. It was no longer safe to let your children wander. Children playing in their neighborhoods without parental guidance quickly become a memory. This was especially true in metropolitan areas. In small towns across America, parents had to be cautious and aware of their children's location at all times.

In the Houston/Galveston area, it became routine to hear of the disappearance of girls. Many of these girls were found murdered and sometimes mutilated. The perpetrator did not bother to bury the victims. The killer or killers would kidnap a young girl, take her to a rural area, sexually assault her, and murder her. These young victims were disposed of like garbage. In Brazoria County alone, over twenty young girls were found dumped in rural areas. One of Brazoria County's first kidnappings and murders occurred on June 17, 1971. Collette Wilson, thirteen, was dropped off after band practice at a rural bus stop by her bandleader near Alvin, Texas. She disappeared. Five months later, her nude body was found about thirty-five miles away in Houston near the dry Addick's Reservoir. Collette had been shot in the head.

The Brazoria County Sheriff cleared Collette's murder administratively with the arrest of two Houston area tow truck drivers, Henry Latham and Tony Knoppa. Although there was no physical evidence connecting them, they were thought responsible for Collette's abduction and murder. Latham and Knoppa were never formally charged in Colette's murder. As it turned out, this was not the only time police temporarily cleared the murder of Collette Wilson with the arrest of a suspect involved in a murder with similarities. Several times, young girl's murders were cleared by the arrest of a suspect with a similar MO. These men were never criminally charged or tried in a court of law. Later the cases were reopened and remain unsolved. This happened over and over. It appeared to some that the police wanted so desperately to clear the unsolved murders—the lack of physical evidence, corroborating statements or confessions' didn't seem to matter.

Galveston County had its first kidnapping and murder of a young girl on July 1, 1971. Brenda Jones, a fourteen-year-old African-American, disappeared while walking home from a

Galveston hospital. Brenda, one of the first victims, was an exception from the killer's pattern. During the first fifteen years of killings, she was the only known African-American victim. The day after her disappearance, Brenda's body was found floating nearby in Galveston Bay, close to Sea World Parkway and Interstate 45. Brenda's body revealed a fatal head wound. Her murder remains unsolved thirty-eight years later. The murders of young girls in Galveston County continued for three and one-half years. The last of the murders occurred on September 6, 1974 when Brooks Bracewell, twelve, and Georgia Geer, fourteen, disappeared from a convenience store in the small community of Dickenson. The girls cut school that day and disappeared. Months later, their bodies were found in Alvin (Brazoria County) Swamp. Both girls were beaten to death. From June 17, 1971 until September 6, 1974, twenty-eight girls were abducted and murdered in the area surrounding southern Harris County, northern Brazoria County, and Galveston County. For unexplained reasons, there was a lull in the rash of "reported" killings for five or six years. Criminal profilers suspected the killer relocated or was incarcerated.

After this lull, the murders resumed with a vengeance on July 1, 1982 when Tamara Ellen McCurry disappeared from Galveston after being seen getting into an orange or yellow van. The murders continued another four years: Heidi Villereal, twenty-three, Sondra Ramber, fourteen, Jane Doe, Laura Lynn Miller, and a headless woman found in Galveston State Park. All the girls' bodies were found except for Sondra Ramber's.

Even though there was a lull in murders reported to authorities, bodies or skeletal remains in and around Houston and Galveston continued to be found with no police press releases. The cases were classified as skeletal remains or grave interruptions, because there was no physical evidence, no names tied to the remains, and most of all, no grieving families. The cases were often shelved with little if any investigation. A killer was getting away with murder without any pressure from law enforcement.

We are focusing on thirteen murders. Some of these crimes have been referred to as the "Killing Fields" murders or the "I-45

Corridor Killings." The modus operandi (MO) of the killer or killers was similar. The location of the victims was of particular note. The unburied bodies were deposited in fields or waterways near main roadways. Many of the victims had been executed by a shot to the head with small caliber gun. The victim's underpants were taken from the crime scene. Many law enforcement investigators believe there is a compelling argument that Charles Hitzfelder Jr. was involved in several of these killings. In the late 1990s, a FBI profiler concluded that the I-45 murders were likely the result of three or four sets of serial killers in the Houston area. In the late 1990s, law enforcement officials finally set up a task force after the "Killing Fields" series. The task force, long since disbanded, achieved only limited success in solving the series of murders. The task force focused on murders occurring in the late 1980s and 1990s. They determined that when murders were fresh, there was a better chance to solve the crime.

The decision to focus on more recent murders may have been politically wise. However, this was a big mistake for one simple reason. If a serial killer started murdering in the early 1970s, and was never caught, what would be his motivation to stop? Some in the FBI believe that serial killers tend to stop their killings when they grow older. I disagree. Once a serial killer takes a life, the power he felt can only be experienced again by killing again. While it makes sense to focus on the most recent cases, there is an obligation by law enforcement to try and solve all of murders in the Houston area with similar method of operations. The task force had eye witnesses and the gruesome images were still fresh in the public's mind. The most important law enforcement development of the twentieth century, DNA testing, was now available. DNA brought into play the possibility of matching crime scenes to suspects.

We feel that the thirteen young girls, whose murders may be connected to Charlie Hitzfelder Jr., reveal an opportunity missed by law enforcement. The victims were mostly taken in and around Galveston and Brazoria counties from October 1971 to the latter part of 1985. Charlie Hitzfelder Jr. lived in the middle of this killing field.

Colette Wilson
Disappeared on June 17, 1971

On June 17, 1971, Colette Anise Wilson vanished. Colette was a student at Dulles High School, which was closed for the summer, but the band was practicing in nearby Sugarland. The day Colette disappeared, her parents arranged for her band teacher to drive her into Alvin, Texas (Brazoria County) after practice. The band leader drove her to a bus stop near State Highway 6 and County Road 99 in Alvin and dropped Collette off. Her mother was expected to meet her at 12:30 P.M. When Colette's mother arrived, she did not see her at the bus stop, but noticed an old black vehicle leaving the area. Colette was 5'2" tall, weighed one hundred pounds, had blue eyes, and wore her long dark hair in a ponytail. She was wearing a white T-shirt with the image of Mickey Mouse on the front, purple shorts and brown "chukka" boots. She was carrying a leather "squaw purse" and a case with her clarinet and sheet music.

Colette Wilson was never seen alive again. Several months later, her nude body was found close to Interstate 10 and Highway 6 in the Houston area near the dry Addick's Reservoir. Colette had been shot in the head with a small caliber weapon, possibly a 22-caliber pistol.

For several months, local police and the sheriff's department kept the disappearance of Colette on the front burner. Brazoria County Sheriff Robert Gladney assigned one of his deputies to coordinate all search efforts. Collette's father, Dr. T.O. Wilson, was a local dentist and very close to his daughter. He took her disappearance hard. The family held twenty-four-hour vigils were people gathered and discussed ways to find Collette. Many different searches were undertaken. Dr Wilson offered a $5,000 reward for information on Colette's whereabouts. Community members raised an additional $5,000. This was a huge sum of money in the early 70s. Colette left behind nine bothers and sisters. The family was devastated.

Over the next few months, searches were conducted around the Wilson house, throughout northern Brazoria County and parts of Houston. The numerous volunteers found no sign of Colette. Months later, Colette's body was found near Addick's Reservoir. Colette's remains were found a mere one hundred yards from where another murdered girl had been found the week before. Hikers in the area came upon the body of Gloria Ann Gonzales. Ms. Gonzales was nineteen and from Houston when she disappeared. By late November, Houston area police agencies were worried that they had a serial killer on their hands. From June to November 1971, police recovered the bodies of five missing girls. The publicity surrounding the abductions and murders were making national news. Police in Houston received hundreds of telephone calls from parents of missing girls from all across the United States.

With all the news coverage, Harris County Sheriff Buster Kern held a meeting with local law enforcement agencies to discuss the series of cases. In 1971, task forces were seldom formed in the law enforcement community. Petty jealousies, suspicions, and mistrust of one another prevented cooperation between different law enforcement agencies. The idea of a joint meeting was a big deal back then. People thought the sheriff was taking these murders very seriously. There was immense pressure on lawmen working the cases. Police started arresting and interviewing likely suspects. Over the next few years, three suspects were arrested for Collette's murder. After a few weeks, the cleared suspect would be released.

In April 1972, a man named Ross Byrne made up a story that he was asleep in the back of a car driven by Sam Garcia when the Wilson murder took place. Harris County Sheriff's Department investigators believed Byrne and flew to Chicago to arrest Sam Garcia. Later, the police decided to give Ross Byrne a polygraph test to verify his statement. Before the polygraph, Byrne announced he made up the story of Garcia's involvement in Colette's murder. Byrne said he was drunk at his home in Montgomery County when the police came to arrest him. His mother had called the police to report he was drunk and out of control. Byrne did not want to go to jail, so he made up the whole story. He had not seen Sam Garcia in three years. As he made up the story, Sam's name just popped into his head. The sheriff immediately filed for a dismissal of charges against Sam Garcia. To Sam Garcia's credit, he did not hold a grudge against Byrne and was glad to be released from jail.

At one point, Houston area police arrested Harry Latham, a tow truck driver, along with Anthony "Tony" Knoppa, also of Houston. Latham and Knoppa were no strangers to law enforcement. They had met in the Harris County Jail. Both had been doing time for brutality to women. They were later charged with Linda Faye Sutherlin's murder and the murder of Adele Crabtree, a sixteen-year-old runaway from Ohio. Latham was also charged with the murder of Gloria Gonzalez. The two were suspected of committing other similar murders. Latham had been convicted in the past of many serial rapes. Latham was charged and tried for the murder of Linda Sutherlin. Upon his arrest, Latham was said to have confessed. A shotgun used in the murder was located in a Houston pawn shop. Both men were convicted. Not long after his conviction, Latham attempted a dramatic escape from the Harris County Jail. He somehow acquired a firearm and was shot and killed during his breakout attempt by Harris County Sheriff's Captain Bill Bond.

The killings of Colette Wilson and Gloria Gonzalez were still in the investigative stage, and Latham, now dead, was never tried for the killings. Many in law enforcement breathed a sigh of relief with the arrest and death of Harry Latham, and the incarceration of Tony Knoppa. The killings of Colette Wilson and Gloria Gonzalez were cleared administratively. Many believe today that Latham or Knoppa were responsible for one or two of the abductions and murders, not the scores of murders attributed to them.

Years later, the notorious Henry Lee Lucas was thought to be responsible for Colette's murder. Lucas took lawmen to Collette's crime scene and shared details of the murder only the perpetrator could know. It was determined later that Henry Lee Lucas had killed several young girls and boys, but had nothing to do with Colette's murder.

Lucas was arrested in Williamson County, Texas, and

eventually confessed to hundreds of murders. Lucas liked the attention he was getting from detectives across the country and confessed to any crime to receive better treatment. However, Lucas was not innocent of committing murder. The decade-old murder of Adam Walsh, the son of John Walsh of "*America's Most Wanted,*" was attributed to Henry Lee Lucas. There is no doubt that Lucas was a serial killer. He was just not as prolific as law enforcement initially wanted to believe. FBI investigators, in reviewing Lucas' confessions, found that law enforcement investigators were outwitted by a man who craved attention, free cigarettes, fast-food, and notoriety.

Prior to this fiasco, Houston City Police arrested Arvin George Lason for the aggravated assault of a twenty-year-old Houston waitress. The police suspected Lason of the Wilson murder, but the case against Lason crumbled a few days later. A lineup was set up for the victim of the assault. The victim and another witness could not identify Lason as the attacker. Lason was administered a polygraph test regarding his involvement in the Wilson murder. Arvin Lason passed the polygraph test and was later released.

During the years after Colette's murder, several suspects were questioned and arrested for Colette's death. Colette's father, still a young man, died a few years after Collette's murder without ever knowing why his daughter was taken and killed.

Brenda Jones
Disappeared on July 2, 1971

On July 2, 1971, thirteen-year-old Brenda Jones left home to visit her aunt who worked at the University Texas Medical Branch Hospital in Galveston. Brenda was seen leaving the hospital to board a bus, presumably to go home. She was last seen alive around 7:00 P.M. when she got off the bus near 34th Street and Avenue I in Galveston. Brenda was wearing a white blouse, a navy blue skirt, and white sandals, which laced up her leg. Brenda's bruised and battered body was found the next day, floating face-down in Galveston Bay near the Pelican Island Bridge. Pelican Bridge painters discovered Brenda's body.

Police were called to the scene and secured Brenda's body about 200 yards from shore and 500 yards west of the Pelican Bridge. Investigators discovered Brenda had been hogged-tied with her hands and feet bound by white plastic laces, apparently from her sandals. The half slip she wore was stuck into her mouth, apparently as a gag. An autopsy determined that Brenda had been sexually assaulted. The cause of her death was listed as a blunt force trauma to the head and strangulation. Police speculated that Brenda had been killed elsewhere and placed onto a boat or pier, and then set upon the water. The investigators concluded that Brenda's body had floated quickly in a westerly direction. Brenda's abduction and murder was different than the others because Brenda was African-American. She wore her hair closely cropped. The other girls, for the most part, were Caucasians with long brown hair.

Even though Brenda was African–American, law enforcement officers in short order told the press that all five of the murders in the area were committed by the same suspect. A month after Brenda was murdered; police announced the arrest of a suspect in Brenda's killing. This unnamed man was released after he presumably passed a polygraph test and provided a solid alibi.

A front-page story in the November 30, 1971 *Galveston Daily News* heralded *Same Killer Seen in Five Slayings*. The Galveston County Sheriff J.B. Kline said he and other law enforcement officers in the Houston and Galveston areas believed one killer might be responsible for all five killings. In November 1971, the public was taking note of these murders. The Galveston Human Relations Commission established a reward fund. In November, over $2,100 was pledged as reward money. Harris County Sheriff C.V. Buster Kerns revealed that his men were looking for a twenty-five-year-old male, who may be responsible for the murders. A suspect was not named leading some to believe the sheriff only said this to calm the ragged nerves of the public. News stories in other Texas publications were at odds with the statements of the Harris County sheriff. An article in the Victoria Advocate quoted

Harris County Sheriff's Captain Charles Goodnight as saying he did not believe the recent deaths were related to the three other murders the Houston and Galveston area. However, the possibility was being investigated. The Victoria Advocate story ran just two days before the *Galveston Daily News* story. Captain Goodnight was in charge of the Harris County Investigative Team, which included Sheriff Buster Kerns and J.B. Kline. There were contradictions because the police were stymied. This was a new breed of killer. This kind of sophisticated murder spree had never before been seen. Throughout the 1950s and 1960s, serial killers were identified only after they were arrested for their murders.

Law enforcement was not prepared to investigate a serial killer. There was no sharing of evidence between police agencies. There were no profilers, no sophisticated crime labs, no databases, and no computers. As the years went by the murders continued, but no suspects were ever convicted of Brenda Jones' murder. The murder of Brenda Jones remains unsolved thirty-eight years later.

Rhonda Johnson and Sharon Shaw (Both 14) Disappeared on August 5, 1971

Rhonda Johnson of Webster and Sharon Shaw of Clear Lake City, Texas were close friends. On August 5, 1971, they decided to go to Galveston for an outing. They were last seen hitchhiking toward Galveston. For months, the girls were listed as missing or as runaways. The friends died together.

On January 3, 1972, Rhonda Johnson's skeletal remains were found in Turner Bayou near Shore Acres in southeast Harris County. On February 17, 1972, the remains of Sharon Shaw were found nearby in the same bayou. The girls were abducted at the beginning of the killing spree. At first, their disappearances were treated as runaways. It was not until Rhonda's remains were found that intense police activity started. There were no suspects and there were no clues. The families were desperate for answers. Webster police had their backs against the wall. There was little they could do to name a suspect.

In late October 1972, nine months after the murders, Webster police had yet to identify any suspects. Webster city councilman and car dealer, Ronnie Shapiro, was related to Rhonda Johnson's family. Outraged that there had been no arrests, Shapiro and the city council fired most of the police department. On Shapiro's recommendation, the city hired Texas Highway Patrolman Don Morris as chief and fellow trooper Tommy Deal as his assistant. Within two weeks, Morris and Deal were somehow able to identify and arrest a suspect in the killings of Rhonda and Sharon.

A Webster gas station attendant, Michael Lloyd Self, twenty-three, was identified as the suspect in these brutal crimes. Self allegedly confessed and was charged in Rhonda and Sharon's murders. It was reported that the only thing police had to connect Michael Self to the crimes was his confession. Michael Self was tried, convicted, and sentenced to life in state prison. During his trial, Self alleged that his confession was obtained by threats of death and physical torture. Both Morris and Deal took the stand and denied these claims. In November 1975, Self's attorney told the *Houston Chronicle* that his client's confession was forced and a fabrication. An investigation was launched, while Self remained in jail.

In 1990, Michael Self died in prison of heart failure. Chief Don Morris and his assistant, Tommy Deal, were arrested soon after Self's conviction for committing several bank robberies in the Houston area. The men were sentenced to federal prison. The Harris County prosecutor considered the murders of Johnson and Shaw solved. Self languished in prison for years. It was not until the 1990s that the law enforcement community finally admitted that the killers of Rhonda Johnson and Sharon Shaw were still at large.

Because of Michael Self's arrest, many investigators were thrown off, no longer linking the series of murders. They thought they had their man. Michael Self spent eighteen years in prison as an innocent man. He died in prison on charges brought against him by crooked policemen who ultimately turned to bank robbery.

Gloria Gonzalez
Disappeared on October 28, 1971

Gloria Gonzalez, nineteen, disappeared from near her home in Houston on October 28, 1971. Off from work this day, Gloria's roommate reported that she last saw Gloria at 6:30 A.M. when the girl friend left for work. Both girls worked for the same company. Around midmorning, Gloria called her roommate and asked her to pick up her check. Police learned that later in the morning, Gloria called her mother to tell her she was going shopping in downtown Houston. Afterwards, Gloria planned to stop by the store where her younger sister worked. That was the last time anyone saw Gloria alive.

Gloria had long dark hair. Although Gloria was older than many of the murdered girls in the Houston area discussed in this novel, her disappearance appeared connected to many of the murders. Gloria's body was found near Addick's Reservoir in west Houston only one hundred yards from where the body of Colette Wilson was later found. Gloria Gonzalez' death was caused by a "blunt force trauma to the head." There was a rope tied around Gloria's neck. It is unlikely that two different killers abducted both girls. Both were taken to almost the exact spot. The odds of these murders being committed by completely different killers is like being struck by lighting and winning a multi-state lottery on the same day. Harry Latham confessed to Gloria's murder, as well as the murders of Colette Wilson and Linda Faye Sutherlin. Harry Latham and Tony Knoppa were arrested in Harris County. Harry Latham was tried and convicted of the Sutherlin murder.

Because Latham was shot dead trying to escape from the Harris County Jail, Law enforcement could no longer interview him, trying to clear other murders. Not much more investigation was put forth on Gloria's murder. Law enforcement cleared the case administratively. The bodies of Colette Wilson and Gloria Gonzalez were found a mere one hundred yards apart. Some in law enforcement credited Latham and Knoppa with the murders, while others are skeptical that Henry Latham and Tony Knoppa committed both crimes. The murder of Gloria Gonzalez remains unsolved.

Alison Craven
Disappeared on November 9, 1971

Twelve-year-old Alison Craven disappeared from her south Houston area home on November 9, 1971. Alison's mother left her home while she went shopping for about one hour. When Alison's mother returned to their apartment near I-45, she found Alison missing. Months later on February 1972, a fifteen-year-old boy walking through an overgrown field in Pearland in Brazoria County came across a gruesome sight. He saw the skeletal remains of a human arm and both hands. He fled the field horrified and called the police. When police arrived, they located some human teeth and a pair of wire-rimmed glasses. Three months after this find, other partial remains, including a human arm, were found in a field near Alison's home. Police openly speculated that both of the sites held portions of the victim's body. The field in Pearland was near I-45 and only five to ten miles from where Alison was last seen alive. Alison's remains were positively identified when her eye doctor confirmed the glasses in the Pearland field were hers.

In May 1972, police indicted Henry Doyle Shuffin for the murder of Alison Craven. The indictment stated Shuffin confessed to the slaying and admitted to kicking, stomping, strangling, cutting, and stabbing Alison. Henry Doyle Shuffin pleaded guilty to the crimes. He was convicted of the torture and murder of Alison Craven, and sentenced to twenty-five years in prison.

In June 1975, Shuffin's attorney filed a motion with the court alleging Shuffin's confession and plea were both coerced. Shuffin's attorney asked for a reversal of his client's conviction. According to Shuffin's attorney, the presiding judge at Shuffin's court hearing made promises to Shuffin before he pled guilty. The judge offered to write a letter on Shuffin's behalf, asking for an early release from prison. The attorney's motion was dismissed, but Shuffin's attorney indicated he would appeal the judge's decision. Henry Doyle Shuffin remained in jail until 1992 when he was paroled. After his parole, there were no further efforts on his appeal. It is possible that Henry Doyle Shuffin killed Alison Craven as his confession asserted. However, many were skeptical of the validity of his confession. The murder of Alison Craven is recorded as solved.

Debbie Ackerman and Maria Johnson Disappeared on November 15, 1971

On Monday, November 15, 1971, Debbie Ackerman and Maria Johnson, both fifteen, disappeared. The girls were good friends and attended Galveston's Ball High School. November 11 was a non-school day, so the girls decided to go shopping in downtown Galveston. Maria Johnson lived four or five blocks from the Galveston Mall. The girls decided to go to the Mall to purchase a birthday present for Maria's boyfriend. The girls were very similar in appearance, both very pretty. They had light brown hair, worn above the shoulder, and olive complexions. Investigators learned that the girls made it to the mall that day.

A clerk remembers seeing them eating at one of the restaurants inside the mall. The girls left the mall at around 1 P.M. and were never seen alive again. Their bodies were found floating in the bay near Turners Bayou by Texas City. The site of their recovery was ten miles from Galveston. Investigators theorized that the girls' bodies had been dropped into the bayou from a small bridge about 50 feet down the bayou. The girls' clothing was missing and never found. Both had been sexually assaulted, bound, and dumped into the water. Both girls' hands and legs were bound. Maria was bound with crab line, and Debbie was bound with men's shoelaces. It was determined that Maria Johnson's cause of death was strangulation. Debbie had been shot twice in the throat and neck area with a 38-

caliber weapon.

Police were able to recover a bullet fragment from Debbie's body. The police said the gun was cheap and probably foreign-made. The night before the girls' bodies were found, Maria Johnson's mother called Maria's boyfriend and asked if he had seen the girls. He had not. It was later determined that Maria's boyfriend was in Freeport, Texas that day and was never considered a suspect. Dee Ackerman, Debbie's mother, years later revealed that she had suspected a man named Doc, who owned a boat moored in the Galveston yacht basin. Dee Ackerman, on her own, connected the girls to Doc from information she received from Maria's boyfriend Bubba.

In Dee's quest to solve her daughter's murder, she learned that a night watchman at the yacht basin remembered Doc's boat leaving the basin around 2 P.M. on the day the girls went missing. Dee Ackerman found this interesting, especially after the girls' bodies were found floating nude in Turners Bayou. Turners Bayou can be accessed by boat from Galveston Bay. Dee Ackerman told her close friends of the connection, as well as police investigators, but the police never pursued the lead. Just ten days after the murders, Doc's boat mysteriously sank. The boat was later raised but never searched by police authorities, in spite of Doc's name being turned over to the police.

In 1972, Webster police believed Michael Lloyd Self was also responsible for the Ackerman and Johnson murders, but he was never charged. It appeared as though the police were trying to clear more murders with the arrest of Michael Self.

In 1978, Edward Bell of Galveston was arrested in Pasadena, Texas. Mr. Bell had a background of exposing himself to girls. In one incident, he got out of his red GMC pickup, naked from the waist down, and walked toward two young girls, ages ten and fourteen. Family members heard the young girls cry out, and came to their aid. Larry Gibbons' mother witnessed Bell's behavior and called her son, who was mowing their lawn.

Larry, twenty-seven, saw Bell nude from the waist down, yelling at the terrified girls. Larry told his mother to call the police and ran toward Bell, confronting him. Bell, seeing Larry coming to the girls' aid, tried to retreat into his truck. Larry reached into the truck and took out the truck's keys. Larry wanted to keep Bell on the scene until the police arrived. Bell got into his truck and pulled out a 22-caliber pistol. He told Larry to give him his keys back, and an argument between the men ensued. Bell fired his pistol at Larry, who was in retreat by then. Bell hit Larry several times.

Larry's horrified mother ran into the street where her son lay motionless. She told Bell the police were on the way and to leave her son alone. Bell told Larry's mother he couldn't leave because her son had his keys. She reached down to the pavement and pulled the keys from her motionless son. She handed the keys to Bell, who walked to his truck and pulled out an M-1 carbine rifle. Bell walked back to Larry, placed the barrel of the rifle on Larry's forehead, and pulled the trigger, killing Larry instantly. Bell then fled the scene.

A short time later, Pasadena officers stopped Bell's truck. He surrendered without resistance. For some unfathomable reason, a Harris County judge granted Edward Bell bail. The judge apparently decided Bell was not a threat to the public's safety. Bell posted ten percent of the $15,000 bail and was released from custody. He promptly went on the run. Bell's flight from justice took him to Panama. Years later, police closed in on Bell. He was extradited back to Harris County.

Bell was tried and convicted of murder and four counts of indecency to a child. He was sentenced to seventy years in prison. Today, he remains in the custody of the Texas Department of Corrections. He is housed at the Jester Unit in Richmond, Texas. Investigators would later suspect Bell of the Ackerman and Johnson murders.

Another possible link between Bell, Ackerman, and Johnson in 1971 was Bell's white van. There were reports that Debbie Ackerman and Maria Johnson may have been seen on that fateful day getting into a white van. But witnesses also reported seeing Debbie and Maria getting into a green truck on their last day.

Edward Howard Bell could be responsible for the murders of Debbie Ackerman and Maria Johnson. Edward Bell wrote a letter to authorities from prison confessing to the Ackerman and Johnson murders, as well as several other similar crimes. However, when investigators showed up at the prison to speak to Bell, he refused to see them. Weather Bell was seeking to clear his conscious or gain notoriety and publicity will never be known. One thing is certain; Bell became an outcast to many of his co-prisoners. Even today, inmates shun convicts who have been brutal to children. Perhaps Bell, in prison for the murder of a twenty-eight-year-old man, feared being known as a child killer. The possible repercussions may have scared him and he backed off his reported confession.

Edward Bell was not the only suspect in the murders of Debbie Ackerman and Maria Johnson. Over the years, anyone suspected of the murder of a young girl in the Houston and Galveston areas was under suspicion by the police for other murders.

In 1971, Charlie Hitzfelder Jr. was picked up and questioned by Texas Ranger Bob Elder in regards to the Ackerman and Johnson murders. It was never clear what prompted Ranger Elder picking up Charlie Hitzfelder for questioning. The bodies of Debbie Ackerman and Maria Johnson were found off Humble Camp Road in Galveston County two miles from Can-Go Trucking, where Charlie Junior worked at the time. Additionally, witnesses reported seeing Debbie and Maria about eight blocks from where Charlie was living in November 1971. Investigators also point out that when police recovered the girls' bodies, their underpants were missing. In 1971, the Texas Department of Public Safety issued a memo announcing that Hitzfelder, a "convicted child rapist" had relocated from California back to Texas.

In 1985, Joe Ackerman, Debbie's father, died. Her mother, Dee Ackerman, passed away in 2005. Dee Ackerman never gave up looking for the killer of her daughter. She kept a thirty-four-year diary of clippings and handwritten notes. The diary was full of her thoughts and hopes of solving this horrible crime. Debbie's parents are now gone, never learning who killed Debbie and Maria.

About three weeks after Debbie Ackerman and Maria Johnson were killed, a note was found inside a public restroom on Galveston's West Beach. The letter stated, "I did not mean to do it.

May God forgive me, "I killed Debbie Ackerman and Maria Johnson".

Police told the press that they had in their possession a similar undisclosed note, also claiming responsibility for the murders of Debbie and Maria. Handwriting expects decided that three different people wrote the note. A news report indicated that police had identified one of the letter's writers, but this person was neither charged nor connected to the crime.

Kimberly Ray Pitchford
Disappeared on January 3, 1973

Sixteen-year-old Kimberly Ray Pitchford was dropped off by her parents at Dobie High School in Pasadena, Texas to attend a driver's education class. Kimberly was supposed to call her parents for a ride home after she completed her class, but she never called. Two days later, on January 5, 1971, her body was found in a ditch by two boys walking along County Road 65, near the small community of Iowa Colony. The location is near SH 288 in Angleton (Brazoria County), Texas. The boys had noticed a jacket hanging on a fence the previous day. Upon returning to the site the following day, the coat was still hanging on the fence, so the boys investigated further. Kimberly's body was observed lying in a ditch, just off the road. Kimberly was wearing the dress she had on when she disappeared. She was missing her shoes and watch. Brazoria County sheriff Investigators responded to the crime scene. No physical evidence was found. An autopsy was ordered by a county justice of the peace.

The results revealed that Kimberly had been sexually assaulted, strangled, and killed. Kimberly's body was found about thirty miles from the Pasadena High School, which she attended. It was clear she was taken to this location and her body discarded. Kimberly's uncle, Ray Pitchford, provided the police with a possible suspect, an alleged serial rapist whom he thought had once attended Kimberly's school. No other suspect was ever publicly identified. The case remains unsolved thirty-six years later.

Georgia Geer and Brooks Bracewell Disappeared on September 6, 1974

Twelve-year-old Brooks Bracewell and fourteen-year-old Georgia Geer decided to skip school on September 6, 1974. They made their way to a Dickenson (Galveston County) convenience store. Witnesses later said the girls were seen using the pay telephone outside the store. Both girls had medium complexions with light brown shoulder-length hair and weighed less than 140 pounds. The girls just disappeared.

Over the next seven years the girls' bodies were not found. Their bodies were found on April 13, 1981 badly decomposed in a remote swampland near Alvin, Texas in Brazoria County. The girls' skulls had two small caliber bullet holes, similar to Carolyn Covey. The bullet holes were consistent with a 22-caliber pistol. Prior to the finding, law enforcement treated the girls' disappearance as runaways. Many complained about the way law enforcement approached the handling of runaway cases. The girls had disappeared around the time of many other disappearances and murders in the area. There is little public information on these crimes. The Houston area newspapers did not run many stories on the murders. Internet sleuth sites list these murders as unsolved.

Sondra Ramber Disappeared on October 25, 1983

Sondra Ramber, fourteen, disappeared from her home in Santa Fe, Texas on October 25, 1983. Sandra was similar in appearance to many of the young murdered girls. She had dark hair and a medium complexion. Twenty-six years later neither Sondra nor her body has been found. Although still listed as missing, most believe she was a victim of a serial killer working in Galveston County from 1971 to 1985.

Charlie Hitzfelder Jr. is directly connected to the disappearance of Sondra Ramber. At the time, Charlie's marriage to Patricia Sweet-Ellis was ending. Charlie molested Patricia's daughter, Francine, during the marriage. Charlie beat Patricia and terrorized the family. Sondra and Francine Ellis' little sister, Eva, were best friends. The two attended the same school. The girls would frequently go skating together. Charlie would often watch them skate. Sondra and Francine's sister played volleyball at school. Charlie Jr. would come to the practices and the games. Charlie knew Sondra. The very day Sondra went missing, Patricia Sweet was dating Sondra's father, Alton. On the day she went missing, Alton came home and saw that the oven was on. Sondra's purse and other things were on a table. Sondra was missing. Alton was worried and called Patricia on the phone. Several people came to his house and looked for Sondra that afternoon. The next day, Alton called the police and reported her missing. We know that Charlie would often follow Patricia's car around when he saw her driving. When Patricia and Charlie had fights, he would try to find her to punish her. Charlie knew about Patricia's relationship with Alton Ramber. He must have known where the Rambers' lived. Sondra knew Charlie from school outings. The two could have met that day—or was this just a fluke?

FOURTEEN
Rogue Cops May Have Hindered Investigations

There was a pivotal event in the early 1970s, which caused investigators to take their focus off the mounting count of young girls murdered in the Houston area. Twenty-three-year-old Webster gas station attendant Michael Lloyd Self was picked up by the new Webster, Texas police chief and his assistant. Self was questioned, and eventually charged with the murders of Rhonda Johnson and Sharon Shaw. Information dissembled to the public through the news media announced that Self had confessed to this horrific crime. Self was tried and convicted for the murders of Johnson and Shaw. Self appealed his conviction.

An investigation conducted years later by the Harris County district attorney found that Self's confession did not support the physical facts and evidence. It was determined that the facts contained in the confession did not add up. Self said he picked up one of the girls at her house on the night of their disappearance. This was not possible. The girls had been reported missing hours before Self allegedly said he picked up the girls. Also, in Self's confession he maintained that he killed the girls by beating them about the head with a Coke bottle. This was not possible. The girls' autopsy report revealed that there were no skull fractures or head injuries that could have been caused by a weapon such as a Coke bottle. Adding further doubt to Self's guilt, the Harris County investigation also uncovered an effort to clean-up inconsistencies in Self's first confession. They learned that just prior to his trial; Self was taken from the Harris County Jail to be re-interviewed. In a new and "improved" interview, Self allegedly changed his confession.

The new confession cleared up some of the inconsistencies seen by the prosecuting attorney. The arrest and conviction played a major role in convincing law enforcement that Self was responsible for at least six other similar murders occurring around this time: Collette Wilson (6/17/71), Brenda Jones (7/1/71), Gloria Gonzalez (10/28/71), Alison Craven (11/9/71), and Debbie Ackerman and Maria Johnson (11/10/71). Investigators working these crimes put these cases on hold because they believed that Self was responsible for the murders under investigation. Law enforcement officers at the time did not know that Self's guilt was in doubt. No one will ever know for certain if the arrest and focus on Michael Self allowed others to get away with murder.

FIFTEEN
The Truth About a Sheriff's Son

In tracking the comings and goings of Charlie Hitzfelder Jr. from 1960 to his death in 1998, a picture developed. Charlie left Hondo, Texas in October 1960 to join the Navy. After Charlie's discharge from the Navy, he married Charlene and lived in Northern California until 1971. After Charlene and Charlie divorced, he remarried and moved to the Galveston, Texas area. Charlie lived and worked in the Galveston area until the mid-1980s. After leaving the Galveston area, Charlie drifted back and forth between Medina County and Arizona driving long-haul trucks. He finally returned to Medina County in the early 1990s, living out the rest of his years. Charlie died in 1998 in the small town of Natalia, Texas.

Putting together Charlie's life, the writer found that Charlie was seen by two Hondo men on February 13, 1961 and February 14, 1961. He was dating Carolyn Covey at the time. Charlie Junior and his family always insisted that he was in San Diego on February 14, 1961. Naval record's neither confirms nor disproves Junior was in San Diego. It would have been easy for him to change his duty with another sailor, giving him nine consecutive days of leave.

In addition to the sightings of Charlie Jr. in Hondo, John Schulte reported that he picked up a girl hitchhiking on Valentine's night, 1961. The girl told Schulte she was going to meet her boyfriend, who was AWOL from the service. The girl also said that her boyfriend was stationed in California, and finally that his father was the local sheriff. It is believed by many that the girl was Carolyn Covey. Pauline Sanchez, a school friend of Carolyn's reports that Carolyn was going to meet her boy friend that night and run away to Louisiana.

While he was in the Navy, Charlie was arrested for the rape of twelve-year-old Sandra Moorefield.

Over the course of many years, two of Charlie's stepdaughters reported repeated sexual abuse and rape at the hands of Charlie. This number of stepdaughters molested by Charlie could actually be three. Charlie's stepdaughters all bore similar appearances. They all were ten to twelve years old when Charlie started molesting them. Many murder victims were very young when they disappeared. Charlie's ex-wives alleged sexual deviancy, including having guns held to their heads, while Charlie demanded sexual intercourse, as he threatened to shoot them. Many victims, including Carolyn Covey, were shot in the head. Charlie was arrested and acquitted of the rape of his ten-year-old stepdaughter.

Charlie reported a burglary to his house in November 1972. He said the thief only took women's underpants. He reported three blood stains inside the house. Many victims had their underpants taken from the crime scenes. Charlie's ex-wife was dating the father of Sondra Ramber on the day she went missing. Charlie had been to many school functions with his stepdaughters and Sondra Ramber. He knew Sondra. The disappearance and murder of Debbie Ackerman and Maria Johnson were strikingly similar to Carolyn Covey's murder. Police report that Debbie and Maria were last seen less than a mile from where Charlie lived at the time. Their bodies were found about two miles from where Charlie worked at the time.

Years later, Charlie was followed to a locked gate leading to the bayou where the girls' bodies were found. Charlie sat and stared in the direction of where the girls were found. Charlie was said to have the keys to many of the gates leading to oil slush fields. Charlie was connected to the skeletal remains of a young unidentified girl found in Manvel, Texas in December 1979. The girl was shot twice in the head. The victim was dumped in a field, much like Carolyn Covey. Charlie owned weapons of the same caliber as those used in several of the murders, namely, a 22-caliber magnum pistol, a 22-caliber rifle, and a 38-caliber pistol.

Many of the victims were found near or in oil field slush pits, rural fields just off highways and in and near bodies of water. It is known that Charlie's job with Can-Go Trucking often took him to several of these slush pits to pump sludge oil. Years afterwards Santa Fe Police learned that Charlie had keys to sites were some of the bodies were found, including the League City "Killing Fields."

Trying to Drum Up Interest in A Possible Serial Killer

When I first started writing this novel, I had long suspected that Charlie Hitzfelder Jr could be a serial killer. My opinion was formed thirty years ago, while investigating the skeletal remains found in Manvel, Texas in December 1979. My subsequent work on this case further raised my suspicions. I left Texas law enforcement in late 1980 after moving to California. I worked another nine years with the San Mateo, California Police Department before retiring. As the years went by, I often thought about Charlie Hitzfelder Jr.

In late 2008, I was provided the opportunity to write this book with the assistance of Sheriff Campsey. I contacted Charlie's ex-wives and former stepchildren. The facts I learned made me want to share my findings with law enforcement officials. Charlie was dead, but there were still families that needed closure. If enough evidence could be corroborated, it could lead to one conclusion: Charlie may have killed many of the girls we have written about. Charlie was directly associated to Sondra Ramber's disappearance and could be responsible. I linked Charlie to the Debbie Ackerman and Maria Johnson killings. I located a 22-caliber rifle owned by Charlie. Many of the girls were shot with a 22-caliber weapon. The pistol Charlie owned for over thirty years was conveniently missing. Those who suspect its dark history may be hiding it. Dolly Buser told me Charlie frequented pawn shops last two years of his life. He was flat broke when he died. He could have pawned a pistol in Medina County. He could have sold it to Dolly's uncle, who worked with Charlie. Dolly could have the gun as well.

Dolly Buser seemed cooperative in March 2009, but accusations by Charlie's sister suggest Dolly or Charlie's sister maybe holding something back. Charlie's sister declined to participate in this story. I made contacts with law enforcement in Texas, intending to provide them with some of my findings. I am an old cop, who wants to help these families end their years of just not knowing and maybe give them some peace.

My contacts with Texas law enforcement were a disappointment. Only one agency seemed interested and wanted to look into what I was telling them. I was totally surprised with the lack of cooperation I received from my old sheriff's department. The Brazoria County sheriff is Charles Wagner. He is life-long lawman with a good reputation. I worked with Charles Wagner in 1978. He was a sergeant with the Freeport Police Department at the time. I was assigned sheriff's patrol in the Freeport/Lake Jackson area.

I called the sheriff directly and he took my call, appearing very attentive and interested. He remembered me from the late 1970s. Sheriff Wagner told me he would fill in the captain in charge of investigations. The sheriff told me to call the captain directly later that day. When I made the call, I felt the captain was not too interested in what I had to say. I assured him that I felt I had facts that could be of assistance. I told the captain that I would be in Brazoria County for four days in March 2009.

When I arrived in Brazoria County, I telephoned the captain. He said he was busy and asked me to call him two days later. I said I would. Two days came and went before I called the captain's office. I was told he was in a meeting. I drove to the county jail in the morning and searched out his secretary. I gave her my card and told her I was there about some old murders. She told me the captain could not be disturbed. I asked if I could wait to see him. She replied that it might be all day or even the next day before he could see me. I got the message. I figured my time in Texas could be better spent than sitting around a lobby for two days. I asked the secretary to have the captain call me on my cellular phone. Months later, I am still waiting for his call. When I returned to California, I sent a letter to Sheriff Wagner telling him I did not meet with his captain. I provided the sheriff with a toll-free number and said I would be available anytime. In the letter, I reported that I had located a 22-caliber rifle owned by Charlie Hitzfelder Jr. The letter got no reaction from anyone in Brazoria County. I know law enforcement is very busy. I know the cases are cold. I just could not understand why the captain would not take ten minutes to listen to what I had to say. I may never know the answer to why I was received that way.

I recently talked with a former fellow investigator from Brazoria County. He said that the "current" leadership in Brazoria County was "not very helpful" when it came to old cases. The Brazoria County sheriff was not the only police agency who seemed disinterested. I called the League City Police, the site of the Killing Field murders, on two occasions. I was told to talk to the captain in charge of investigations. I left the man two messages. I also sent him a detailed e-mail. The fact that Charlie had a key to the gates of the Killing Fields should have been of interest to him. Today, I continue to wait to hear from the League City Police.

I contacted officials with the Galveston County Sheriff's Department and spoke with a high ranking detective. He was too busy to see me. I spoke with a Texas Ranger, one of two who work on "cold" murder cases. The ranger was polite and told me he would get back to me. He never did. I pretty much had the same kind of treatment from the Harris County Sheriff's Department. They seemed like real nice people and their cold-case murder unit was just reforming. Maybe this was why I never received a call back from them.

This book was written for one purpose and one purpose only. Sheriff Campsey and I feel that the Covey family and the other families should finally have peace. They deserve to know what really happened to Claudette in 1961 and to their daughters. We have gone to great lengths to try to stay neutral and hold our opinions to ourselves. Today, I conclude that Charlie Hitzfelder Jr. was involved in the killing of Claudette Carolyn Covey in 1961. I also believe it is possible that someone connected to his family helped kill Carolyn. I interviewed every living spouse of Charlie. There are seven women still alive today. I also spoke to the families of the two women who are deceased. Five of these women remember Charlie as a cruel and violent man, a man who often beat his wives for little or no reason. Some described him as a sexual pervert. Some of his stepchildren say he was a child molester.

We know that Charlie was arrested twice in his life for having sexual intercourse with twelve-year-old girls. We know the vast majority of victims killed in the Galveston and Houston areas were as young as twelve. We know that several of the victims were shot in the head with a pistol, as was Carolyn. The victims' bodies were often dumped in fields along roadways. Their bodies were not buried, just like Carolyn. I have drawn a connection with Charlie to the Ackerman and Johnson murders. I have directly connected him to the unknown skeletal remains found in Manvel, Texas in 1979. Charlie is directly connected to Sondra Ramber and her disappearance. Charlie was said to have access to the Killing Fields in League City, where four girls' bodies were dumped. Charlie liked to point his gun at the heads of his women. He talked of killing one of his wife's and getting away with the Covey murder. We know that Charlie owned guns similar to those used in the murders. We know that some of the victims were violently beaten, just as Charlie had beaten his wives and stepchildren for many years.

Finally, we know that Charlie confessed to beating Juanita Hutto-Lamb badly on the day of her death, withholding medical treatment for hours. Charlie Jr. bragged to Dolly Buser that he "beat the case" when referring to the Carolyn Covey murder. In the last few years of Charlie's life, he apparently settled down, if the women in the last few years of his life are to be believed. If these women were telling the truth, after Charlie's divorce from Debbie Biggs in 1985, he became a gentleman, something it took him a lifetime to accomplish.

We truly hope that the publication of this book will prompt law enforcement to take another hard look at their unsolved cases. Justice for some families may finally be found.

ACKNOWLEDGEMENTS

There are many people I would like to thank for helping me write this book. First, the book could never have been written without the years of dedication by Sheriff Butch Campsey. He spent many years of his life trying to find the truth and solve the Claudette Carolyn Covey murder. I think Butch himself would agree that Carolyn's murder had a major impact on his life for the past thirty-five years. Carolyn's murder was at the forefront of his personal life for many years. Why else would Butch carry Carolyn's remains with him everywhere he went? The banker's box, containing files about her murder, was just as precious to Butch as Carolyn's remains. Carolyn's death consumed him. I want to thank him for his dedication to solving Carolyn's murder and for allowing me to write her story.

I acknowledge Bill Butler for all his assistance to Butch and me over the years. Bill works full time as a pharmacist, but over the years he found many hours to volunteer as a deputy sheriff. Thanks to Bill's son, Bart Butler, and Tony Ramey for writing Carolyn's song, *The Wrong Way Out*. Carolyn's sisters and I love this song.

If it were not for Melanie Thomson, my long-time secretary, who donated many hours on the initial editing of this book, it would still be a dream.

I would like to thank Gordon Sievert Jr. Gordon and I went to the Police Academy together twenty-nine years ago. Prior to coming to law enforcement, Gordon was an English teacher at San Mateo High School. Gordon has retired from the San Mateo Police Department and now runs the College of San Mateo's Regional Police Academy. Gordon wields a mighty pen. I remember academy instructors speaking to him on the subject of writing police reports. Gordon took on the challenge of editing this work.

My thanks go out to Captain Wayne Kessler of the Santa Fe Police Department in Texas. Wayne has been investigating murders and other serious crimes for decades. He is a top-of-the-line investigator. Wayne was there for me, and without his friendship, I would be lost.

Finally, Eddie Barr needs to be acknowledged. Eddie spent thirty years in law enforcement on Galveston Island before serving as a county commissioner. Now, Eddie works at the Galveston Yacht Club, continuing his lifelong passion of boating. Eddie was, and still is, one hell of a lawman. He excelled in the profession. At one point, he was the Galveston police chief, a County Commissioner and Lord knows what other high positions he held. Eddie, Butch, and I had our suspicions about the sheriff's son thirty years ago. Eddie spent countless hours trying to solve several murders which we thought were committed by the son. In writing this book, Eddie was there for me again.

SHERIFF CAMPSEY WOULD LIKE TO ACKNOWLEDGE

Bill Butler and I first met in 1976 while I was campaigning for Medina County sheriff. I didn't know it at the time, but Bill and I would become lifelong friends. Bill volunteered many hours of work on several criminal cases between 1977 and 1984. Bill and I still visit from time to time, but not nearly as much as I would like to.

Chief Adult and Juvenile Probation Officer Frank Perkins and I first met when I took office in 1977. Frank was always ready and willing to jump right in and help the sheriff's department, and did so many times. Frank later went to work at the Hondo Independent School District. He now serves the community as a school counselor.

Dorothy Beard passed on to be with her heavenly family a number of years ago. I can't say enough about how much she meant to me and everyone else that worked with her. Dorothy worked as a dispatcher, a secretary, and even a jailer for the sheriff's department. Sometimes, Dorothy performed all three jobs at the same time. I will always miss her.

I would like to thank Earl Heath, Richard Wells, Tommy Goslin, and Steve Hannemann. These men held the fort together while Bill, Frank, and I went out of county to work on the Covey murder. I hired these young men believing they had good hearts and good common sense. All four men made me proud and proved my belief in them to be right. After leaving the sheriff's department, all went on to bigger and better things. Earl became a Texas Highway Patrolman. Richard went to work for Sheriff Tommy Williams in Atascosa County. Tommy is, in my opinion, the best and most respected sheriff in the State of Texas. Tommy Goslin later worked for the sheriff's department in Victoria, Texas. He went on to become a high ranking member of the department. Steve went to work for the Texas Health Department and rapidly moved up the ranks. All of these young men made me proud to have been associated with them.

Last but not least, my thanks go to Wayne Skarka. I met Wayne in February 1980. Wayne and I became friends and have remained friends for almost three decades. I formed an opinion very quickly that he was a can-do person and was sincere about solving criminal cases, particular murders of young victims. I would especially like to thank Wayne for believing and recognizing the importance of telling this story. Thank you for the immense amount of time you have spent in writing this book.

WORKS CITED

Alameda County, CA. Adult Probation Dept. Oakland. *Probation Report: Chas Hitzfelder Jr.* By C. Daniel Estorga. 70051st ed. Vol. F-249. Print.

"Ancestry.com." *Texas Birth Records*. Web. Nov.-Dec. 2008. <http://ancestry.com>.

"Arthur Campsey Interview." Interview by Donald Campsey. Print.

"Beverly Hutto-Interview." Interview by Eddie Barr. Print.

Bishop, Jim. "Search Goes On for Slayer(s) of Girls." *The Houston Post* [Houston, Texas] 18 June 1972: 23-C. Print.

"Body Found Though to Be Hondo Girl." *Denton Record-Chronicle* [Denton, Texas] 02 Nov. 1961, sec. 2: 1. Print.

"Body Identification Anticipated." *Galveston Daily News* [Galveston, Texas] 28 Feb. 1972: A-1. Print.

"Body of Missing Alvin Girl Found." *The Baytown Sun* [Baytown, Texas] 28 Nov. 1971: A-1--2. Print.

"Bullet Tested for Clues in Girls Death." *Houston Post* [Houston, Texas] 01 Jan. 1973. Print.

Burglary, residential-11/03/1972. Galveston Co SO. Print.

"Butch Campsey." Interview by Wayne S. Skarka. *Corrupt Sheriff*. Print.

"Charlene Fisher-Interview." Telephone Interview.

"Chief Jerry Blinka-Interview." Interview by Donald Campsey. Print.

"Covey Slaying Still a Mystery." *San Antonio Express* [San Antonio, Texas] 08 Nov. 1962: 22-B. Print.

"CV-61 USS Ranger Reunion Site." *USS Ranger CV-6-Historical and Memorial Website*. Web. 02 Feb. 2009.

Deal, Jerry. "Body of Missing Hondo Girl Found." *San Antonio Express* [San Antonio, Texas] 02 Nov. 1961, Final ed., Front Page sec.: 1-3-A. Print.

"Death Master File." *Death Master File-Texas*. 01 Jan. 2009.

Web. 17 Jan. 2009. <http://merlindata.com>.

"Debra Jo Biggs-Interview." Telephone interview. 05 July 2009.

"Dennis Heyen Interview." Telephone interview. 05 May 2009.

"Denver Police Quiz Kidnap Suspect About Four Deaths." *Galveston Daily News* [Galveston, Texas] 27 Dec. 1961: 3. Print.

"Dolly Buser-Interview." Personal interview. 10 Mar. 2009.

"Ellie Mae Holskey." Telephone interview. 08 Jan. 2009.

"Faye Bokkean-Interview." Telephone interview. 05 May 2009.

Herman, Lee. "Bodies of 2 Dickenson Girls Found." *Galveston Daily News* [Galveston, Texas] 05 Apr. 1981: 2-A. Print.

Hevener, Paul. "She Was my Daughter, Saddened Father Says." *Houston Post* [Houston, Texas] 19 Nov. 1971. Print.

"The I-45 Corridor Killings." *Unsolved Serial Killings*. Web. 05 Apr. 2009.

"The I-45 Victims." *Tri-pod.com*. Tri-Pod-Serial Killers. Web. 20 Jan. 09.

"Investigators Hunt Similarities in Murders of 21 Young Girls." *Del Rio News Herald* [Del Rio, Texas] 06 Apr. 1981: 3. Print.

"Joe Duran." Personal interview. 16 Dec. 1979.

"Joe Fohn Interview." Interview by Donald Campsey. Print.

"John Q. Sailor-Interview." Telephone interview. 07 Jan. 2009.

"John Shulte Interview." Interview by Donald Campsey. Print.

"Julie Covey-Interview." Interview by Donald Campsey. Print.

Kennedy, Tommy. "Family Praying for Some Word of Missing Girl." *Houston Post* [Houston, Texas] 18 July 1971. Print.

"Linda Duran." Personal interview. 16 Dec. 1979.

"Link Sought in Slayings of 40 Young Texas Girls." *San Antonio Express News* [San Antonio, Texas] 6 Apr. 1981, Street Final ed., Front Page sec.: 1. Print.

"Link Sought in Slayings." *Victoria Advocate* [Victoria, Texas] 01 Jan. 1973: 8-A. Print.

Lyons, David. "Coeds Last Seen Alive- 1 Year Ago." *Galveston Daily News* [Galveston, Texas] 18 Nov. 1972: 1. Print.

Lyons, David. “Murders of 2 Galveston Girls Remained Unsolved.” *Galveston Daily News* [Galveston, Texas] 17 Nov. 1973: A-1+. Print.

“Man Charged in Deaths of Pair of Young Girls.” *The Odessa American* [Odessa, Texas] 10 June 1972: 3-A. Print.

“Man Charged, Questioned in Another Murder.” *The Brazosport Facts* [Freeport, Texas] 11 June 1971: 24-24. Print.

Marby, Paul. “Body of 2nd Slain Girl Found.” *Galveston Daily News* [Galveston, Texas] 19 Nov. 1971: 1-A-4-A. Print.

“Mary Ruth Cadenhead.” Telephone interview. 03 Mar. 2009.

Mitchell, Doug. “Memory of Missing Girls Will Live On--Along I-45.” *Galveston Daily News* [Galveston, Texas] 18 Sept. 2002, Opinion sec.: A-8--9. Print.

“No Leads in Double Killing.” *Galveston Daily News* 25 Nov. 1971: A-1. Print.

“Officers Probe Calls in Covey Girl Case.” *San Antonio Express* [San Antonio, Texas] 03 Nov. 1961, 8-A sec.: 8-8. Print.

“Pauline Sanchez Interview.” Interview by Donald Campsey. Print.

Pickard, Breck. “Till Death Do Us Part.” *Galveston County Police News* Jan. 2007: 1+. Print.

Pickard, Richard. “Missing Girls 1973-1999 Harris County.” *Crimesearch.net*. Crime Search Research and Analysis. Web. 25 Jan. 2009.

“Police To Quiz Accused Killer in Slaying of Girl.” *El Paso Herald-Post* [El Paso, Texas] 02 Nov. 1961: 27. Print.

“Police Try to Link 21 Murders.” *The Paris News* [Paris, Texas] 06 Apr. 1981: 3. Print.

Porter, Breck. "Detective convinced imprisoned Killer Murdered Six Area Girls.” *Galveston County Police News* Aug. 2006: 1+. Print.

Porter, Breck. “Murder Investigation Likely Marred By Crooked Cops.” *Galveston County Police News* Oct. 2006: 1+. Print.

Porter, Breck. “Person of Interest NOT Interested.” *Galveston County Police News* June 2006: 1+. Print.

Porter, Breck. “Police have “Person of Interest” in '71 Double

Murder." *Galveston County Police News* May 2006: 1-2. Print.

Porter, Breck. "The Memoirs of A Cop, Matt Wingo." *Galveston County Police News* Aug. 2007: 1+. Print.

Price, Jorjanna. "Same Killer Seen in 5 Slayings." *Galveston Daily News* [Galveston, Texas] 30 Nov. 1971: A-1--12. Print.

"Protect The Kids.Com." *Angelfire.com*. Protect the Kids Com. Web. 20 Jan. 2009.

"Rancher Finds Body of Woman on Range." *Valley Morning Star* [Harlingen, Texas] 4 Feb. 1952: 1-1. Print.

"Ranger H. Joaquin Jackson." Telephone interview. Jan.-Feb. 1980.

"Report Awaited." *Galveston Daily News* [Galveston, Texas] 28 Mar. 1981: 5-A. Print.

"Sherry Yates-Interview." Telephone interview. 04 May 2009.

"Shirley Covey-Interview." Telephone interview. 08 June 2009.

Simon, Janice. "Unsolved Mysteries." *Galveston Co. Daily News* [Galveston, Texas] 13 Jan. 1991, Lifestyle sec.: D-1--15. Print.

Skarka, Wayne M., comp. *City of Alameda, CA police records*. NA, 1963. Print.

Skarka, Wayne M. *Handbook of Texas Online*. *The Handbook of Texas Online*. Web. 21 Dec. 2008. <http://www.tahaonine./org/handbook>.

Skarka, Wayne M. US Naval Records. Raw data. Review of Public Records.

"Slain Girls Identified." *Syracuse Post-Standard* [Syracuse, New York] 07 Apr. 1981: A-6. Print.

Stanton, Robert. "Unsolved Murders—No arrests made in at Least 25 County Homicides." *Galveston Daily News* 20 Sept. 1987: 1-A-5-A. Print.

State of California Vs. Chas Hitzfelder. NA Public Recs 1-5. Alameda Co. Municipal Court. Aug.-Sept. 1953. Print.

"Steven Hutto-Interview." Interview by Eddie Barr. Print.

"Suspect Quizzed in Hondo Slaying." *San Antonio Express* 27 Dec. 1961, Alfred Rathoff ed.: 1. Print.

"Suspect Quizzing Widened." *Galveston Daily News*

[Galveston, Texas] 6 Nov. 1972, Michael Lloyd Self ed., Passing Parade sec.: A-1--1. Print.

Sweet, Frances. "Patricia Sweet." Telephone interview. 10 Dec. 2008.

"Teen Murder Case--Suspects Cleared." *Galveston Daily News* [Galveston, Texas] 25 Mar. 1974: 1-A. Print.

"35 Things we Love About Texas." *Texas Highways, The travel Magazine of Travel*. Texas Highway Department. Web. 4 Aug. 2009.

Thompson, Paul. "Missing Girl"- Covey. *San Antonio Express News* 08 Apr. 1961, Top of the News sec.: 1-1. Print.

Thompson, Paul. "Paul Thompson Column: "Poor Charlie"" *San Antonio Express News* [San Antonio, TX] 02 Sept. 1973. Print.

"Wayne Kessler." Telephone interview. Mar. 2009.

Williams, Scott. "35 Years and Holding: Detective Probes 1971 Murders." *Galveston Daily News* [Galveston, Texas] 19 Nov. 2006: A-1+. Print.

LaVergne, TN USA
07 June 2010
185320LV00001B/22/P